The Color Of SUSPICION

Best Wishes
Thank You,
Shawn Boal

The Color Of SUSPICION

The Demise of the Inner City Family

Shawn M Boal

Library of Congress Control Number: 2011903716
ISBN: Hardcover   978-1-4568-8340-9
               Softcover   978-1-4568-8339-3
               Ebook   978-1-4568-8341-6

This book was printed in the United States of America.

To order additional copies of this book, contact:
Xlibris Corporation
1-888-795-4274
www.Xlibris.com
Orders@Xlibris.com
90693

Contents

This book is dedicated to my loving mother, Patricia Caetta.

Acknowledgments:

*May God bless my dear friends Hasani Ngozi,
Dan Radca, Brice Gindratt,
William Suggett, Mark Bindus, Chris Davis,
Jim Mousetes, William Carter,
Anthony Grimes, Allen Fite, Tom Conway,
Craig Lake, and James Holmgren.*

Special thanks to:

*My sisters Sara Boal, Christi Schaber, Kelly Smith,
my brother Jonathan Boal, and father James Boal*

* Great appreciation to first run editor Ann Hagedorn.

I am like a tame bonfire with loved ones gathered around
But can rage if too many things are placed upon me
You must respect my devastating capabilities
So you can enjoy my warmth and hospitality
But don't get too close because the fire holds its boundaries
However, I will allow you subtly in to cook nourishing foods
But will burn you and cause you to draw back if you touch me
You can move my flames slightly with the wind
But I will always draw back to home
You can try to smother me out and extinguish my existence
But I will smoke in anger and scoff at you
And when our battle is complete and you have terminated my life
You and your loved ones will always come back and revive me
To be both loved and hated again.

Shawn M. Boal

Chapter 1

Introduction

The demise of the family structure within the inner city has never been more prevalent than today. Increased violence within the inner city across the nation has led to a rise in divorce, strained police relations, juvenile delinquency, and crime. Many sociologists and other theorists focus on one specific reason for this demise as it relates to their profession or personal beliefs. Others may give their point of view while looking out the bay window of their suburban home within their gated community. Many of these individuals are college educated but lack the firsthand experience of either being raised in the inner city or extensively working within the inner city, which is crucial to fully understand the many factors straining the family system. I have gained a vast amount of knowledge relating to the inner-city family by being raised within the heart of an inner city, being college educated within that city, and then working as a police officer and police sergeant in that same city for over fourteen years.

I was born and grew up in the inner city of Akron, Ohio, which has a similar economy makeup of Cleveland due to the close proximity of the two cities being less than fifty miles apart. Akron has a population of slightly greater than 200,000 people, which is compromised of approximately 63 percent Caucasian and 31 percent African-American (BestPlaces.net 2010). My parents always told me stories of how in the 1960s and '70s, Akron was the rubber capital of the world and jobs were plentiful. They stated that people brought their families to Akron from all over the United States to seek employment in the booming town. I was born in 1972 at the tail end of the rubber industry boom. Today, most of the old tire making buildings sit vacant, or are operated by a small skeleton crew. Many of the tire-making factories moved south, taking their jobs with them and leaving families in a state of flux. I never saw the days here my parents spoke about where jobs and money were plentiful and the financial strain families endure was less burdensome.

When I grew up in Akron, my mother raised five children including myself in a small three-bedroom house deep in the inner city. My friends, of course, all grew up in the same neighborhood and were subject to the same financial strife as my family. Government cheese was as common in our refrigerator as the luxury of a two-car garage is in the suburbs.

All my friends' parents received food stamps, although this is something we rarely discussed unless it was to tease each other when our parents forced us to go to the store and buy groceries with them. All of my friends in my neighborhood, including myself, came from single-parent homes. Most of our parents were either working hard to support us, using drugs, or were just too busy for us. We shared clothes, food, stories, and whatever else we had together. My mother worked very hard at her job to make sure we always had a place to call home. She did her best to provide for us and to show us that she cared and that we mattered by expressing her love for us every day. However, as a single parent with five children, my mother's job stretched our family time thin. With no help from my father, my mother was forced to compromise our time to grow together in order to earn money to provide our basic needs. Without my father involved in my life and my mother working outside the home in order for us to survive, I turned to my friends to fulfill the remaining emotional support I needed. My friends and I developed a close friendship and bond that offered us a support system outside of our strained family structure. We learned that in order to avoid getting assaulted, robbed, or downright killed in our neighborhood, you needed to have respect. Respect among your peers was probably and still is the most sought after thing within the inner city. It is hard to attain a lot of money and material things within the inner city through legitimate means; however, everyone has the opportunity to obtain respect. Respect among us came in the form of group cohesion. We stuck together and formed a bond that allowed us the opportunity to be ourselves within that group. We were able to express our ideas, goals, family problems, and interests with each other.

From the outside, if an individual drove by and observed about ten of us routinely sitting on one of our front porches talking about sports, they may believe, at first glance, that we were a gang. When hanging out together in a large group in the city, it is easy to get mislabeled as a gang. To constitute a gang, we lacked what many kids that just hang out together lack, which is the element of criminal activity within the group. We achieved respect among our peers through our close bond. Everyone knew that if one individual experienced a problem outside the group, we would stand behind that individual and help him any way we could. At times it meant physically fighting to protect the person, but that was not the group's purpose of its existence. It was a form of support among a group of youths who lacked the skill of being able to verbally defuse an escalated problem. I remember an incident when I was fourteen years old and my mother's boyfriend disciplined me and went too far and left bruising on my face. The next day, one of my close friends saw my face and inquired about what had happened. Always feeling close to my group of friends, I shared what had transpired the night before with him. That same evening, I was home when I received a knock at the door from my close friend. After opening the door, I observed my friend standing there with about fourteen other friends of mine. They were all very upset and agitated about what had happened to me. My mother's boyfriend was not at the house yet, but they insisted on staying there and confronting him about the incident. Out of respect for my mother and her choice to be with him, I convinced my friends to leave and not pursue the matter. If an individual outside our group witnessed this incident or just observed our group walking down the street, many individuals may just lock their car doors and label us a violent street gang as they drive past to their destination.

For every wrong label placed on an individual or group, there is a door of opportunity closed to them out of fear or misunderstanding. For example, if you were eager to invest your money in stocks during the stock market boom in 1998 but did not trust black people and labeled them as con artists or thieves, then you probably would have closed a door of opportunity if a young black stockbroker approached you in the hallway of a hotel business seminar to speak to you about a potentially lucrative stock hitting the market called eBay. The odds are based on your stereotypes and mislabeling; you probably would have scurried by him acting like you were talking on your cell phone while trying not to make eye contact. Stereotypes and mislabeling can lead to missed opportunities for both parties involved. An employer who stereotypes a potential job applicant and passes over him based on his or her own stereotypes, risks losing a potential future employee of the year, manager, or CEO. The job applicant therefore loses the opportunity to succeed, buy that wedding ring, support his or her family, and achieve a sense of self-worth.

I personally have gained an enormous amount of knowledge and understanding about the family structure within the inner city and the difficulties people face by not only growing up in one, but by also interacting with families as a police officer and listening to their problems. I tried to solve their problems and offer solutions while maintaining a nonjudgmental point of view. Just as easy as it is for the individual to lock his car doors driving down the street and mislabel the group of teens hanging out as a violent gang; it is just as easy, if not easier, for me to mislabel and stereotype the many families who call the police every day as helpless. Unlike many police officers that routinely answered calls jaded, cynical, and judgmental, I maintained a nonjudgmental view that allowed the citizens and myself to have an open line of communication. This open line of communication gave me the opportunity to learn about the many problems facing inner-city families in today's complex society. In the upcoming chapters, I will explore the many different strains put on inner-city families. Some of these strains examined will be the direct cause of police policies and procedures and some will be an indirect result stemming from police culture. Other strains I will explore look at the inner-city family structure itself and the social support services within the community. You will see that without police changes, family support, parental ownership, and wholehearted community involvement, the demise of the inner-city family is inevitable.

My childhood, like so many others in the inner city, was filled with frustration about my surroundings outside my group of friends. I rarely saw my father who I so desperately wanted and needed to have in my life. Growing up in the 1980s, no matter what part of the country you grew up in, or how tough you claimed to be; everyone seemed to watch *The Cosby Show*. A Huxtable-style family was portrayed as the American family. I think everyone within our group would have traded places with Theo Huxtable in order to be part of the Huxtable family. It was not that we did not love our mothers or other family members, but we were frustrated that our fathers were not playing an instrumental role in our lives as we saw Heathcliff Huxtable playing in Theo's life. Individuals within our group choose to express this frustration in different ways. Some would run away from home, while others would focus all their time and energy on sports. Many of my friends used the football field as a way to vent and release their bottled-up frustration through legal physical contact. Whatever the means were it was important that we found legitimate ways to let our frustration out. I choose to vent in a very different manner than my friends who mostly played football to relieve themselves from the frustration of their everyday life. I choose to isolate myself in my room, in the woods, or on top of my garage, and write or daydream about my desire to have both my mother and father raising me in my home.

One summer, I was faced with my daydreams and consuming desire to have a stable life with both parents together and involved in my life. During the summer of 1987, I was fifteen years old and interested in making some spending money with a few of my friends. We ended up spending our evenings and weekends selling chocolates, peanut brittle, and fudge door to door to help support a local youth group. We got to keep a dollar for every box we sold for ourselves. It was not a challenge to sell a lot of candy. I usually sold the most in the group, mostly to elderly women who would pinch my cheeks and call me names like "cutie" or "sweetie." Our group was always driven to the suburbs to sell our candy in order to better our chances of selling more by reaching a richer clientele.

The challenge for me came after routinely ringing the doorbell of a beautiful suburban home where I was frequently greeted by a mother, father, and their children. This is what I saw on television, what I wrote about, what I daydreamed about, what I wanted, and I saw firsthand that it was real. It was the life that I had so desperately wanted and desired ever since my father became predominately absent from my life following my parents' divorce when I was eleven years old. Even at only fifteen years old, I knew that I was only looking at the structure of the family while selling candy, and that they probably had their own stresses and problems within their family. The structure is what I wanted, and the best thing was that I did not know what strains and problems they had. Therefore, I could picture my life living in a beautiful suburban house with a mother, father, and siblings. Then I could envision a loving family the way I wanted it to be.

For several weeks, I observed the family structure that I wanted and daydreamed about a family that I did not have. This time I did not become frustrated, but I became depressed. Soon every time I went to the suburbs with my group to sell candy, it was the same experience for me. I would walk down the neat neighborhood sidewalks, holding my cardboard box filled with candy, and cry. I was unable to bring myself to approach any of the houses because I knew that I would probably be confronted with the one thing I so dearly wanted—a father. Throughout my childhood and my young adult life, I always associated a nice house in the suburbs with a father. Primarily because fathers were rare in the inner-city neighborhood I grew up in and this was my first personal experience of routinely seeing fathers in a family setting.

While in high school, I never saw education as a tool to succeed economically in life and obtain a quiet house in the suburbs that I knew existed. I lacked interest in academics and although I had the capability, I did not wish to excel in any subject. I did just enough to pass each class with minimal effort. During my high school years, like most teenagers, I wanted a role model in my life for guidance, self-fulfillment, and someone to look up to. Like most teens, I was open and susceptible to be easily influenced by my peers. Without a father to guide me and place me in an environment or situation where I would interact with positive role models, I was left open to being influenced by negative role models outside of my group.

Our group was very strong and the tightly-knit bond that seemed indestructible during our early teen years was under intense strain from many outside factors during our late teen years. Many of my friends within the group succumbed to the coercion of local street gangs and became members. Other friends within my group began to experiment with drugs, some becoming addicted while going down a troublesome path of hardship and despair. The reality of what was occurring in our lives was very troublesome to me. I grew up with all of the individuals in our group and considered them my family. We shared all of our feelings and ambitions together. I knew my friends wanted to become pro athletes, doctors, musicians, and lawyers. They did not aspire to be drug users and street gang members. I knew something was wrong as our group was quickly deteriorating, but I did not know what was causing most of my friends to choose such destructive lives.

Looking back now at the separate paths my friends chose, I can see that the lack of positive male role models within our own neighborhood led to many of my friends' poor choices regarding their future. I knew their goals and dreams were the same as any other person their age. They desired the same occupational fields as any other child regardless of color or class. When growing up within an inner city, survival is a matter of guidance, resilience, or just plain luck. It takes a very durable and focused youth who can, by him or herself, fend off the multitude of negative influences seeping its way through every crack of the inner-city family foundation. The more dysfunctional the family, the more cracks in its foundation, the greater number of problems the individuals within the family will endure. The odds of a youth successfully mending every crack and building a stable foundation to establish him or herself is enormously against them. In order for the youth to succeed and build a foundation complete with all the necessary morals, values, emotional and rational thinking needed to help them succeed in life, they need guidance. The youths who have no guidance from at least one parent or role model are far less likely to achieve both financial and emotional stability than a youth who has at least one individual providing them with guidance. Most of us within our group, as well as numerous other youths within the city who learned the tools and was given the emotional support necessary to function successfully in society, were taught these valuable tools by either our mother, grandparent(s), or sibling(s). I often wonder how many more youths would have been strong enough to fight off the negative influences and succeed if more of our fathers were involved in our lives.

Sometimes in our youth the individuals we come across who serve as role models to us occur by chance from within the environment we place ourselves. For example, when I was seventeen years old, I joined a bodybuilding gym within the city. The gym was inside a decaying building that used to be a dancer bar several years prior. The gym owner converted an old wooden dancer stage into an area for power lifters to conduct strength-training exercises such as dead lifts and squats. Next to the wooden stage sat an outdated floor model radio whose station knobs were frequently fought for control of by the many sweat-dripping muscular men who worked out in the facility. Within six months I discovered that there were many drug users within the gym. These were not the street drugs such as crack and marijuana that came with negative terms such as "crackhead" and "pothead" which several friends from my group began using. These were anabolic steroids, which made these men bigger, faster, and stronger. These drugs gave the men a significant edge over the non-using gym members like myself, not to mention they also had women flocking to squeeze their rippling biceps. Anabolic steroid usage was very common in the gym and frequently observed. Often I would open the door to the humid, stench filled locker room and observe an individual injecting himself with a steroid filled syringe in his buttocks.

At seventeen years old I was very small in stature being 5'10" and only weighing a frail 130 lbs. I wanted to transform my slender body into a masculine shaped body that would increase my strength, muscle mass, and physical appearance. Although I knew many of the weightlifters were illegally using anabolic steroids, I was still looking for a role model to fill a void in my life left vacant by my father. Even though I knew many of the individuals at the gym were attaining the muscle and strength I desired illegally, I still had an admiration for the muscular stature they had achieved. Just as the many fans did who overlooked baseball great Sammy Sosa's use of an illegally corked bat and steroid use, and instead focused on his accomplishments during baseball's steroid era. I overlooked the illegal steroid use within the gym and instead marveled in the end result of their masculinity.

I wanted to attain a physique similar to theirs and I was captivated by the respect they received in the community based on their physique. I attended several neighborhood festivals and would also go out to eat on occasion with several steroid users in our gym. At these functions, numerous people would compliment the individuals from my gym on their outstanding muscular shape. At this point I was beginning to gravitate toward their lifestyle and become persuaded by witnessing all of the attention they were receiving. I started to hang around them more and began to work out with a few of the steroid users at the gym. I started to earn their trust and one day I was asked, in the gym locker room, by one of my workout partners if I wanted to buy any anabolic steroids from him. Before I could answer, a college student named Mark who worked at the gym walked in and asked me if I could help him move an exercise machine. I agreed to help Mark and by chance I was taken out of the potentially disastrous situation and placed into a positive setting that could grow and flourish.

After helping Mark move the machine, he began to inquire about my future goals. In the past, I spoke to Mark on several occasions briefly and the extent of our conversations never went beyond a mere polite inquiry of how the other person was doing. I shrugged my skinny shoulders and advised Mark that I only had given thought of entering the military after high school. Mark looked at me puzzled and asked if I had explored other options besides the military. He then informed me that he was attending the University of Akron and was pursuing a four-year degree. He asked me what I wanted to be in life. I answered the question the same way I had when asked several other times during my youth by my teachers, parents, and friends. I told Mark that I wished to become a police officer. Mark then questioned me about how I planned to accomplish my job career goal and reach my destination by enlisting in the military. Mark's curiosity about my future caused me to come to the reality that I had never devised a plan in my life of how I was actually going to become a police officer. When growing up teachers, parents, and friends frequently asked what you want to be in life; but they never asked what my plan to get there was. Unlike a captain of a ship who strategically maps out the route to his desired destination, I knew what final outcome I wanted but never concocted a plan to reach the goal. Without a plan I would undoubtedly drift aimlessly throughout life. If I managed to overcome a trial or problem, I would never progress closer to my goal of becoming a police officer because I did not have a planned route to follow. With no definite plan, Mark began to inform me of the many degrees the University of Akron offered relating to the law enforcement field.

For the first time in my life, I began to formulate a plan on how I was going to reach my career goals. It was by chance that Mark came into my life that day and unknowingly steered me away from the negative gym members who were beginning to influence my life in a manner that offered no focus or real self-fulfillment in life. Mark was in great shape; in fact, his body structure was more proportionate than the drug abusing weight partners I had associated with. Mark chose to reach a muscular level of excellence not by using steroids, but by eating healthy and focusing on the discipline of consistently working out. I would soon learn that Mark worked out very intense five times a week and rarely missed a workout. He was pursuing a degree to become a dietician and used his knowledge in the field to construct a healthy diet of consuming nutritious foods. That day we became workout partners and, more importantly, friends. Mark also created a diet for me to follow that concentrated on the consumption of nutritious foods such as chicken and tuna fish that would help build my desired muscle mass. Mark was both insightful to various career opportunities and compassionate in his willingness to help others. He could easily be defined as a leader to anyone who envied his disciplined lifestyle and illuminating sense of class. Mark, who was four years older than me, became not only my friend but my role model.

Through Mark's encouragement, leadership, and support I enrolled in college at the University of Akron in June of 1991. Although I only achieved a 2.0 grade point average in high school, I was sure that I could follow Mark's path. I had started to believe in myself and my ability, because when I interacted with Mark, I could see that I was able to follow him and mimic many of his qualities in his character. I knew that if Mark could succeed at school, the groundwork was already laid and all I had to do was follow the path he took. I felt that if I completed school, I could one day reside in a beautiful suburban home that I associated with having a father in the household.

I then focused all of my energy on graduating from college. I elected to pursue an associate degree in Criminal Justice and a bachelor's degree in Sociology/Corrections. I had an unsettling desire to succeed scholastically like Mark, become a police officer, and purchase a suburban home to raise a family.

While in school, I applied my newly learned self-discipline from the gym to my studies and immediately began to thrive academically. The first three years I made the dean's list every semester by obtaining a grade point average of over 3.0. My confidence was rising each semester and the better I did in school, the greater my hunger for knowledge grew. For the first time in my life, I was excelling academically at the top of every class I took. I can recall being called a "nerd" by classmates in several classes after they consistently observed my high test scores in challenging subjects. During my childhood, I had never eclipsed the realm of educational excellence to be categorized as a "nerd" or a "geek." The classroom teasing could be taken as an insult to many individuals; however, I considered the terms used in the teasing as a compliment that my hard work was being noticed.

In August of 1995, I graduated from the University of Akron with an associate and a bachelor's degree. I also achieved a 3.3 overall grade point average through my effort and perseverance and became the first person in my family to graduate from college. At the graduation ceremony, I felt a sense of peace and fulfillment. I had found an inner peace with myself knowing that my mother's sacrifices she made while raising five rambunctious children in a small house was not in vain. I felt that her hard work and sacrifices that she made in her life in order to raise us could be measured as a success when I graduated from college. When I accepted my diplomas I knew in my heart that I was accepting them on behalf of both of us. I could then use my degrees as a key to open many doors to job opportunities that required a four-year degree. Once inside, I planned to use the knowledge I acquired throughout life to assist me in performing my job in a fair and unbiased manner to all individuals I encountered regardless of race or class.

Three weeks after graduating from college I accepted a job as a police officer for the City of Akron in August of 1995. From the first day of the training academy until the end of my career in 2010, I served the community I grew up in with pride and respect. During my years of service I received multiple commendations and compliments from my superiors for my investigations and police actions in cases involving homicides, aggravated burglaries, carjackings, rapes, felonious assaults, drug arrests, and various other calls for service. While serving as a police officer for twelve years and a police sergeant for three years, I was selected as a field training officer, a community crisis intervention team member, given an award for fit for duty officer of the month, and achieved all high marks on semiannual performance evaluations. My desire to help people extended beyond the fabric of my police uniform. I had volunteered my time for eleven years mentoring a youth, whose father was not involved in his life, through United Way's Big Brother Big Sister Program. During my career as a police officer, I also volunteered my time at a local hospital's spiritual health center. This gave me the chance to visit the rooms of newly-admitted patients and be there for them for spiritual support if they needed to confide in me any fears or concerns they were having regarding their upcoming medical procedure or religious uncertainties. In 2005, I traveled to Ecuador on a medical mission trip with several members of my church. The group consisted of four medical doctors, five dentists, twelve nurses, and approximately twenty other general skilled, good-hearted people eager to help the citizens of Ecuador. We set up a work site inside a local church and through our efforts, working under God's supervision, we successfully treated 1,400 desolate people during our week-long stay. We provided much needed medical, dental, and vision care to people who otherwise could not afford the treatment. After arriving back in the States, I was so moved by the impact we had on the lives we touched through medical missions that I decided to enroll in nursing school in pursuit of my registered nursing (RN) degree. My enrollment in nursing school was based solely on emotions and my desire to continue to passionately work and contribute more to the medical mission field. I had no idea going into the program just how much studying, dedication, and organization it would take to become a nurse. For the next five years I found myself studying four hours every day, attending four-hour class sessions, three-hour labs, completing case studies, figuring out the lab workups on my patients as it related to their medical diagnosis, and treating my patients in clinical. I continued to work and after five years and thousands of hours of sacrificed sleep and diligence of a strict mindset, I achieved my RN degree in May of 2010.

My duties as a field training officer enabled me to train new rookie police officers after they graduate from the police academy. I was able to instill my police ethics and knowledge in the officer while training him or her to be a professional officer. It was always my pleasure to train a new officer because I knew that I was helping them build a foundation in the law enforcement field that they would have throughout their career. My responsibilities were both immense and intense. In six short months, I had to educate the rookie officer in many areas including officer safety, current laws and procedures, community relations, ethics, and detailed report writing. If I failed to teach the rookie officer these skills, it could result in the officer being fired before he completes his probation period or it may even result in his death, or another officer's death due to an error in safety techniques. For example, when I was a rookie, my training officer, William Suggett, always emphasized the importance of mastering the gun retention skills that we were taught in the academy, and to have compassion for the individuals and their family that we encountered. Officer Suggett encouraged me to continually practice the gun retention training and always stressed the fact that more officers were killed in the line of duty each year by the suspects taking the officer's gun, than from the suspect's own personal weapon. I complied with Officer Suggett's request and routinely practiced gun retention techniques off duty with other officers from my academy class. Officer Suggett's persistent emphasis on gun retention training caused me to improve my skills and undoubtedly saved my life on several occasions during my career. As a rookie officer, I was not fully aware of the many vicious suspects I would encounter who would attempt to assault me out of anger, or in hope to flee from me to avoid being arrested. I can honestly say that I was ignorant to the constant dangers of the job and greatly underestimated the number of people willing to assault or attempt to kill a police officer in the line of duty.

On one occasion while working patrol, I was dispatched to an apartment in order to bring a mentally-ill individual back to a mental health facility that he walked away from before being treated by a doctor. After arriving on scene, I observed that the individual's front door to his apartment was forced open. The door was open into the apartment's living room and wood was splintered away from the door. The dead bolt was broken off the door and was lying on the ground at the base of the door. I observed the mentally-ill individual sitting on his living room couch. The individual was an African-American male in his midthirties and was approximately 6'0" tall and well over 200 lbs. as his shoulders and arms were extremely muscular as his striations were clearly visible from the gray tank top we wore that clung to his well-built frame. Upon entering the apartment, the individual immediately stood up and ran toward me with his head down and fists clinched while swinging his arms wildly in an attempt to assault me. Although I was struck by his flying fists on my head and shoulder area, I managed to quickly sidestep to my right to avoid behind knocked to the ground by the charging assailant. The attacker ignored my order to cease because he was under arrest and turned toward me and lunged his body in the direction of my duty gun. His sudden rush allowed him to wrap both of his hands around the grip of my handgun, which was still in the holster. The assailant began forcefully tugging on the grip of my handgun while shouting, "Just kill me! I am going to kill us all!" With each desperate pull of my handgun by the attacker, my body rocked forward making it difficult to maintain my balance. I remember thinking to myself, as the mentally-ill man struggled for my handgun, that these are the circumstances where officers are actually killed in the line of duty and never return home to their loved ones. Just then, I could feel my blood racing toward my left eye where I was punched when I heard the pop of my holster snap come undone. I was quickly aware that the assailant had managed to get my gun halfway out of the holster as I desperately fought to push the weapon back down into the holster and break free from his grasp. It was now a reality that I could be murdered with my own gun.

Under such a stressful condition I could feel my heart rate drastically increase as my hands and arms began to quiver from the rush of adrenaline my body was releasing. The room grew smaller and the crackling sound of my leather holster being tugged at became quieter as my visual and audio perception began to be overcome by my body attempting to compensate for the stressful condition. I resorted to my encouraged gun retention training to defend myself. The repetitive training allowed me to rely on muscle memory training skills that I executed almost subconsciously. In fear for my life, I lowered my base, which increased my balance by squatting down approximately six inches and spreading my feet shoulder width apart. I was then able to regain my balance even though the attacker still continued to pull on my handgun. With each forceful pull I could feel the gun rattle back and forth in the unsecure holster as I frantically tried to resecure the gun in my holster. I continued to execute my training methods by having my hands clamped down overtop of the assailant's hands in order to secure my gun in the holster. Instead of attempting to pry the attacker's fingers away from my holster, my training taught me to focus on his forearms to cause his grip to be released. With my left hand, I began to strike the attacker's forearms using a karate chop technique. The strikes caused the assailant to release his grip and allowed me to establish enough space between us to resecure my handgun and pepper spray the attacker. Although the pepper spray struck the subject directly in the face, this did not affect the attacker in any way to subdue him; instead it only seemed to incite his violent behavior. The attacker began to yell, "I am going to slaughter you," as he ran over to a nearby window and slammed his head into the window causing the glass to shatter and plunge to the ground while bouncing off of the carpet and reflecting sharp rays of sunshine-like diamonds. The attacker ran over and wrapped his arms around my back as he attempted to overpower me and slam me onto the ground. Again I lowered my base and positioned my left leg outside of his right leg in order to block his effort to take me off of my feet. I was face to face with the assailant as we each struggled to gain control of each other. When his head brushed against my face, the pepper spray from him transferred to my face causing my vision to become blurry and my eyes to severely sting. The attacker then unclenched his hands from around my back and struck me three times on the left side of my face with a closed fist. The punches jolted my head and upper torso but I managed to push the attacker against a nearby recliner, which we both fell over onto the ground next to the shattered window. Once on the ground, the suspect grabbed onto my gun again and this time attempted to manually undo the holster snap. I quickly punched the suspect's right forearm and then without delay pushed the back of his right shoulder into the ground causing him to be positioned face down on the carpet. I immediately placed myself on the attacker's back and held him down.

Finally, I was able to radio to our dispatcher that I needed help. Sweat, mixed with pepper spray, dripped from my brow onto the back of the suspect's neck as I tiredly waited for another officer to arrive. Although it was only a few minutes before backup officers arrived to help me place the attacker in handcuffs, it seemed like an eternity; as I laid there on top of him and watched my orange-colored sweat roll off of the back of the suspect's next onto the diamond studded carpet. After arresting the mentally-ill individual I was approached by an elderly gentleman who identified himself as the father of the arrested subject. He was concerned about his son's well-being and what was going to happen to him. Although I was assaulted by his son, I took the time to explain to him what had occurred and advised him that I would recommend that his son have a mental health evaluation. I conducted myself professionally and did not take the assault personal. Therefore, I was able to have compassion for both the arrested individual and his father, in order to make the appropriate mental health recommendation. The officer safety techniques and compassion for citizens that Officer Suggett emphasized during my training period are now passed down by myself to eager new rookie officers. I know that if I am able to instill a sense of compassion and respect in the rookie officers for the citizens they encounter, then they will be able to effectively handle calls such as domestic violence and have a positive impact on the victim and their family members involved.

As a community crises intervention team member, I was one of a select group of officers who were interviewed, rated, and hand selected based on character and leadership skills for the team. After being selected as a team member, each officer must complete a forty-hour course of advance training in understanding and interacting with mentally-ill citizens. Since many of the calls a city police officer responds to involves a mentally-ill individual, the increased knowledge and understanding that I learned in the course gave me additional de-escalation techniques that I could use on the job. I have used many of the verbal de-escalation techniques to effectively interact with irate mentally-ill individuals on calls in order to calm the person down and resolve the situation in a peaceful manner, without resorting to other means such as pepper spray or using the Taser.

I frequently observed other patrol officers who were not crises intervention team members become frustrated during an interaction with a mentally-ill individual. The officer usually lacked patience or compassion to effectively deal with the mentally-ill person. Therefore, the officer was usually very quick to find a reason to arrest the person in order to not address the communication barrier. I have learned that this type of action by the officer does not solve the mentally-ill person's problem, nor will he or she find the proper mental health help they need in jail. Without addressing the problem and referring the individual to the proper health support agency, the person will likely have contact with the police again as their dilemma continues unresolved until a responding officer recognizes the mental health issues and makes the correct referrals.

By being a community crises intervention team member, I became aware that many family disputes had an underlying mental health concern. When responding to calls involving acts of domestic violence, most officers seemed to focus only on the facts of the case. The officers go into the call with tunnel vision and are only concerned with the material evidence such as what type of physical violence occurred, if any, and if there were any witnesses. I have found that with the wide variety of stresses family members endure, the topic of the argument before the physical violence occurred was usually not the direct reason for the violence. If an individual assaults a family member or another individual, he deserves to pay his debt to society and serve prison time, if justified. However, if it is determined that the arrested person is mentally ill, then the individual should receive monitored treatment in prison and/or court ordered treatment upon his release from prison. If the individual's treatment is successful, they will be able to better adapt and function in a family setting by dealing with the root of their problem. This will allow the individual and family other resources to use in future stressful conditions that may arise.

Chapter 2

Police vs. Community Relations

A good relationship between the police and public is crucial in order for communities to effectively function and families to strive. Without the community's trust in local law enforcement, there cannot be an open channel of communication between the families within these communities and the police. The strained channel of communication causes both the police department and the families they protect to suffer. Lack of police trust can lead to circumstances such as a child being afraid to approach an officer to report their parent(s) abusing them, citizens who witness crimes not wanting to get involved, and a lack of qualified minorities willing to become police applicants. On the other hand, lack of community support for law enforcement may cause officers to become detached from the citizens they protect, leading the officers to isolate themselves from the public. The isolation may develop into feelings of loneliness and despair. The officers will then bring these unresolved mental health issues with them to work when dealing with and making decisions concerning citizens. If the feelings go unresolved, the officer's issues may cause them to make poor decisions when deciding if a citizen should be arrested. An unjust arrest will surely cause unwanted stress within the family of the person arrested creating turmoil within the family. If officers do not address their mental health issues, extreme circumstances may occur such as an officer mistakenly shooting an innocent citizen during a dangerous scenario such as an armed robbery, or the officer may fall into such a state of despondency that he commits suicide. These drastic measures are not unrealistic and actually occur in today's society.

Tense police relations with the inner-city minority families have been a persistent problem long before the Rodney King incident. While performing my duties as a police officer, I have heard many elderly African-American citizens complain to me about their concern of the possible misuse of my department's K-9 dogs. One elderly African-American gentleman shared a personal experience with me that he had with police dogs during the Civil Rights movement. The elder vividly described with tears in his eyes how a police dog, on command from his handler charged a crowd of peaceful demonstrators that he was part of during a rally in the south. The dog charged the crowd like a bull with no fear, and rapidly approached his friend who he was next to in the crowd. The dog instinctively sprang off the hot pavement and lunged in the air toward his friend's neck. His friend abruptly put his left arm up in a desperate attempt to shield himself from the attack. The police dog sank his teeth into his friend's left forearm causing him to fall backward onto the ground. Upon striking the hard black top, the dog maintained a hold of his friend's forearm and began to shake his head violently back and forth as a stream of blood steadily rolled down the uneven pavement from the back of his head. I still recall the elderly man wiping tears from his eyes while graphically describing the eerie sound of hearing his friend's forearm skin tearing over the dog's unsettling growl.

In order to help his friend, the elderly man said that he intuitively straddled the dog's body with his legs and choked the dog around its neck with both of his hands. He stated that the dog began shaking its head back and forth more savagely while growling louder. He could now see flesh and muscle being wrestled away from bone, as the dog managed to keep its saliva-dripping jaws locked down on his friend's forearm. The elderly man stated that he shifted all of his body weight to his left causing both the dog and himself to fall down onto their sides. The dog gave out a loud yelp and released his friend's bloody forearm. He could see his friend's blood steadily drip from the dog's gums and teeth and then disappear into the black top as he maintained his tight grasp on the dog's neck. His friend managed to stand up and run, with his left arm dangling, through the parking lot and into the dense nearby woods. The elderly man saw the K-9 handler advancing toward him with his nightstick raised in his right hand. He instantaneously released his grasp from the dog and leaped to his feet. The dog, in a state of disarray, retreated and allowed him to bolt across the parking lot and into the woods to safety.

The traumatized individuals who were part of these unforgettable incidents do not forget horrible experiences with police and K-9 dogs such as this. Individuals pass these real-life stories down from generation to generation which allows the police dog handling misconduct they experienced to remain fresh in the minds of many African-American individuals. African-American individuals of all age groups have approached me at sometime in my career and expressed their strong opposition of our K-9 unit. Most of the citizens mentioned the misuse of police dogs during the Civil Rights movement as the basis for their beliefs.

Today, I strongly believe that there are two barriers that must be overcome in order to strengthen the understanding of police department's role in efficiently using K-9 dogs and the community's benefits to allow its use. First, the community must be educated regarding the professional level of training K-9 handlers and their dogs are subjected to. I know that the training on our department is very intense and rigorous, also our department regulates when and how the dogs can be used through written procedures. The dogs also have to pass tate-certified course in order to work on the street. These s have been devised and developed to ensure that the past police dog handling improprieties do not reoccur. Therefore, the dogs can be used as an effective tool in assisting officers in areas such as building searches, drug searches, and locating missing persons and suspects by their scent. One problem of my department was that although the K-9 handlers received excellent training and their dogs were state certified, the supervisors outside the unit did nothing to promote these facts to the public and give them a better understanding of today's K-9 unit. With visions of the misuse of police K-9 dogs still in the minds of many inner-city citizens, K-9 handlers felt the resistance of not being embraced as a police asset by many citizens and city council members. The K-9 handlers faced undiplomatic editorials and verbal slandering by citizens on calls. Finally, the K-9 handlers became exhausted in waiting for police supervision to assist in improving public relations between their unit and the public so they took action themselves. The K-9 handlers began going to schools and workplaces in order to put on live police dog demonstrations. These dog demonstrations showed the dog's discipline in finding hidden drugs which the K-9 handler would hide, and the dog's ability to be called back just before he leaped to bite his attacker (which was another K-9 handler in a padded suit). One K-9 handler frequently enrolled his dog into a Frisbee-catching contest. His dog would receive loud cheers from the crowd as he would routinely leap several feet in the air to bring down the plastic floating object in his mouth. Actions like these allowed the citizens to observe how both trained and friendly the police dogs were. Soon the K-9 handlers were receiving several hundred phone calls a year by citizens to request that they put on a K-9 demonstration at an event. Through their efforts, the handlers also built a personal relationship with community members and gave the K-9 unit a positive persona, which enabled them to work while having much-needed community support.

Another barrier that must be overcome to strengthen the understanding of the police department is that police departments must take into account that the K-9 handler is human and his or her judgment is subject to error, stereotypes, and any personal biases which may arise. Therefore, K-9 handler recruitment should be a very selective process, which examines the officer's desire to be a handler, citizen complaint and use of force history, and the administration of a psychological test. The appointment process should be vigorous because the K-9 handler will always have the dog at his disposal, which should be considered an extra weapon that can be used against a citizen. Those conducting the selection process must understand that officers are not robots who enforce the laws with no feelings or discretion. Every officer has his own beliefs and values that are instilled in them. The most professional officers are able to perform their job at a high level of excellence because they are routinely able to distinguish between their own personal feelings and beliefs that may affect their decision-making process when dealing with citizens in the line of duty. However, this can never happen 100 percent of the time due to so many different personal outside factors affecting even the most professional officers at any given time. Through my experience I have observed that every officer, through certain types of interactions or experiences, is capable of allowing an event or personal situation such as a death or divorce, to trigger his of her own personal feelings that override the training and departmental procedure guiding how the officer should handle the incident. I have observed officers to allow things such as their ego, temper, or deep-rooted personal beliefs to dictate how they handled a call and treated the citizen(s). Therefore, when selecting a K-9 handler they should be meticulously chosen by taking into consideration their past citizen interactions, motivation for the position, ability to maintain professionalism under stress, and personal bias toward the community they protect.

Group mentality can also play a role in community relations, when officers are together on a call, the majority of officers act in a different manner from the way they were trained and how they customarily act on calls by themselves or with a regular partner. In a group, officers become less sensitive toward the citizens' problems they are dealing with. Most officers' egos override the citizens' issues at hand, and the officer's attitude recurrently takes them in a direction that focuses on unproductive sarcasm regarding the nature of the call, or can even lead to desensitized violence within the group of officers toward a labeled suspect. Usually outside of the citizen's hearing range, officers will congregate after handling a call and frequently belittle the caller, the suspect, or the nature of the call through insensitive jokes. In harsh cases such as a homicide, suicide, or other violent crime, officers (myself included), use this form of merciless humor as a way to disconnect from becoming too emotionally attached to the call. The presence of a group of officers on a call can desensitize the group and lead to improper decision-making techniques that violate police procedure, moral standards, and the citizen's civil rights. The mixture of several officers' egos and personal insecurities can supersede proper police conduct if there are no forms of supervision or leadership present. For example, I was working with my partner one evening when we arrived on scene of a heinous motorcycle accident involving a husband and wife who were both on the bike. The motorcycle was on top of the husband who laid against the curb while fighting to breathe through his faint shallow breaths. The wife was lying face down on the pavement and her earlobes were touching the ground as the bone structure of her face had given way to the impact of the solid roadway. The left side of her head was bleeding profusely onto a mixed salad of bone fragments and brain matter that lay on the pavement. After EMS had transported the husband and wife to the hospital where they were pronounced dead, we were waiting for our highway maintenance crew to arrive on scene to clean up victims' blood and body matter. Several citizens had come out of their residences and were either congregating together on the sidewalk or on nearby porches. Four officers and myself were standing in the street talking when my partner, looking at a nearby house, observed a resident wearing a white and pink cotton nightgown, standing on her front porch with several kittens playing at her feet. My partner said in a discourteous voice, but in a volume only loud enough to be heard by the officers, "Hey, lady, why don't you bring your kittens down here and have them lick these brains up." These techniques help officers grieve and express themselves when observing tragic death. However, the real misfortune is that officers are forced to resort to these forms of measures because the macho culture of police departments do not encourage or provide an environment which facilitates expressing their fears. In addition, some police departments, including mine, recently eliminated its Employee Assistance Program due to budget cuts, leaving officers fewer resources to deal with their psychological crises when seeing trauma victims.

It is important to understand the unspoken brotherhood among police officers in order to fully grasp how improprieties of justice against citizens—such as the Rodney King incident—can occur and go unreported among officers. The ability to comprehend the fellowship among officers allows citizens the ability to ascertain why it is infrequent and dangerous for a trustworthy officer to come forward after witnessing an act of injustice by their comrades. The tight bond among police officers goes far beyond the in-cruiser relationship of two partners, but extends into the entire ranks of its paramilitary style structure.

A police department has many divisions and subdivisions within its structure. For example, the investigative unit consists of a detective bureau division that is comprised of various subdivision units such as homicide, burglary, auto theft, and juvenile divisions. Each division has detectives who are specially trained to investigate crimes specifically relating to their unit. The patrol division, on the other hand, consists of several different overlapping shifts of police officers. These officers usually work in marked police cars, are trained to handle a wide variety of calls for service, and enforce criminal and traffic laws. All of the department shifts overlap and work together; therefore, immense pressure is put on each officer to conform to the police subculture of not telling on each other, sticking together, and boosting about causing an injury to a suspect they were apprehending.

Within each subdivision, officers and detectives work closely together and develop a bond of loyalty and respect among each other. When working together to build cases against suspects an *Us vs. Them* mentality that is preached to young rookie officers in the police academy is reinforced. Officers and detectives put a lot of time into cases by tracking down and interviewing potential witnesses, viewing video surveillance, and obtaining search warrants. The enormous amount of man-hours put in by officers and detectives on these cases cause them to take the cases personal. Soon the suspects are seen as the enemy and treatment toward them is rarely just. Some unwarranted acts by officers I observed in my career include a handcuffed prisoner slapped in the face, a defenseless arrested party struck in the head and testicles with a flashlight that I will discuss later, and a citizen choked and his head slammed into the side of a transport wagon, all by over aggressive officers.

The close alliance officers and detectives have toward each other is valuable to rely on when an officer needs backup during a physical fight with a culprit. However, I have observed that over time the officer or detective's perception of trust becomes jaded and they rarely trust the citizens they encounter. This leads to a breakdown in communication between the police and the public because as officers continue to treat citizens poorly, the citizens are less likely to volunteer valuable information which may help solve crimes. Even more disturbing is the fact that statistically speaking, in most major cities, those responsible for a disproportionate amount of crimes are minorities. Therefore, if the detectives and officers are spending a tremendous amount of time investigating minority suspects, then they are more likely to develop racial stereotypes and biases toward that group. I observed an excellent example of this when I worked patrol on the midnight shift. Being that my department was an inner city in the northeast, the majority of our suspects were African-American. Overtime this hindered relationships between African-American and white officers on my shift. I routinely heard white officers complain that they were sick of African-American victims calling the police and also committing crimes in disproportionate numbers to whites. I also heard African-American officers disclose that they would not enforce traffic laws or lower level criminal laws against African-Americans because they felt white officers were already being too hard on African-American citizens. This dissension within our own police department caused segregation on our shift. During our shift, the African-American officers always ate at a separate restaurant from the white officers unless there was a multiracial car. Furthermore at the end of the shift, the African-American officers took the back elevators to exit the building and the white officers took the front. I used to always wonder how we, as officers, could consistently and objectively go on a domestic call involving a white female and African-American male and reach an unbiased decision on how the call should be handled when we could not even work together in harmony with our coworkers of a different race.

Throughout my almost fifteen-year career on the department, I observed many officers take out their egotistical ways, insecurities, negative racial stereotypes, or own family problems on the citizens whom we swore to protect. One of the most common occurrences I routinely viewed on calls occurred when an officer would immediately mock the suspect or victim's current situation. I frequently observed officers mock a citizen's living conditions although they were working well over forty hours a week at a low-paying factory job while attempting to provide for three scrawny children; the officers felt the need to make cruel comments such as, "Is this the best you can do?" or "Children Services will be raising your kids soon." The officers that engaged in this type of demeaning ridicule did not rely on the training method I instilled in my rookie officers of allowing the citizen's actions and attitude to dictate how you treat them. Instead, these officers would prejudge and stereotype the citizen before any dialogue could even occur and the officers would antagonize the citizen based on his or her deep-rooted pessimistic beliefs. Working under this strategy causes the citizen to instantly be on the defense leading to less cooperation with authorities and a possible physical skirmish if the officer repeatedly shows the citizen a lack of his or her desired respect.

Several officers would enjoy stripping the suspect of his respect following a foot chase that resulted in an arrest. The clothing style among inner-city youth is to wear a white colored T-shirt with baggy jeans. During a foot chase with officers, it is common that the youth's jeans will fall down to his ankles allowing the slower officer to take him into custody.

I habitually observed officers slowly walking the suspect out from behind a house and right down the middle of the street toward the cruiser, while the suspect shuffled his feet back and forth as his jeans still clanged to his ankles. The suspect's pleas for the officer to pull up his pants would go blatantly ignored and the half-naked suspect would be paraded to the cruiser in front of neighborhood onlookers.

Through my career, I also witnessed officers become so enraged with a personnel vendetta against a suspect that they damaged the citizen's personal property. For instance, on one occasion I was working with a white officer when we initiated a traffic stop on a young African-American male. The youth abruptly ran from his vehicle and we chased him. After looking for the young male who was exceptionally fast, we notified the responding units that we called off the foot chase and were back en-route to the scene in order to tow the youth's vehicle. While waiting for the tow truck to arrive, my partner was visibly upset because the young male had avoided arrest. My partner punched the cruiser dashboard a few times while yelling, "I'll show that n—r who is boss." My infuriated partner approached the youth's abandoned vehicle and punched the vehicle's stereo face causing the glass to crack in multiple directions. He then removed his canister of pepper spray from his belt and shook the can as I asked, "What are you doing?" My partner looked at me with a cunning grin and stated, "Giving him something to remember us by when he turns on his air," as he sprayed several bursts of pepper spray into the vehicle's vents.

The breakdown of police and community relations can extend further that the mere injustices police officers administer in the areas of verbal insults and the destruction of citizen's physical property. I have personally witnessed numerous unwarranted physical assaults by officers against either handcuffed or nonresisting suspects. These incidents appalled me because my conscience knew it was wrong, our training told us it was wrong, yet officers praised each other for participating in an incident involving a mob mentality. Furthermore, I can recall that every incident in my career—which I observed involving a susceptible and unjustifiable use of force—involved an African-American suspect and all white officers. For instance, a group of officers and myself were involved in a foot chase in pursuit of a young African-American male who had several felony warrants for his arrest. After an exhausting chase during a hot humid summer evening, one of our speedy officers managed to tackle the fleeing youth behind a garage as he attempted to scale a nearby fence. This allowed four other pursuing officers and myself to jump onto the suspect. Commonly referred to as a "pig pile" in the police culture, when these occur, the force used by the officers is rarely reasonable. On most occasions, the "pig pile" consists of several officers—as in this case five officers—jumping on top of the suspect and repeatedly striking the suspect with closed fists while driving your knees into the side of his ribs or femur. The suspect pleaded for us to stop; however, we made sure that citizens in the vicinity could not hear his cries for help as several officers yelled, "Stop resisting. Show us your hands." The suspect, who was not offering any form of resistance, kept his hands open and out to his side as the officers requested. However, within the police lifestyle it was accepted customary to physically pummel any suspect who runs from you. Officers would mask their physical aggression toward the suspect by shouting things such as, "Stop resisting," that causes a bystander to focus on the suspect's movements instead of the physical strikes being inflicted by the officers. By doing this—as in the case where the youth ran from us—the witnesses psychologically believed the young man was resisting arrest although five officers were bombarding him with punches and knee strikes as the youth desperately attempted to surrender. In an effort to stop the onslaught, I squeezed myself between two officers while turning my body sideways in order to avoid being struck by their flurry of punches. Without further ado, I grabbed the youth's hands and placed them behind his back. I removed my handcuffs from my belt and hurriedly placed the youth's wrists in handcuffs. After the incident, I was chastised by the four officers because they stated I had handcuffed the youth too soon. The officers were visibly agitated by my actions as they rolled their eyes and would not help me assist the youth up off of the ground. After placing the arrested youth inside the cruiser, one officer went out of his way to approach me and whisper, "When you run from the police you get beat then arrested, in that order."

During another experience, three officers and myself became involved in a physical struggle with an individual who had just thrown his girlfriend through a glass table. The suspect refused orders to place his hands behind his back and continued to pull his arms away from me and the officers on scene when we attempted to take him into custody. The suspect repeatedly ignored orders to comply and continued breaking free of our grasp. Finally, because there was glass on the floor and the female needed medical attention, one of the officers delivered a closed fist strike to the suspect's head causing a laceration to his forehead. Without delay, blood gushed from the suspect's head placing him in a state of shock. Reality quickly set in and the suspect stopped his resistance without delay and placed his hands behind his back in order to allow us to handcuff him. I removed my handcuffs and placed one handcuff on his left wrist; however, before I could place the second handcuff on the unemotional suspect, another officer pulled out his canister of pepper spray and administered a burst of the agitating chemical directly in the laceration to the suspect's forehead. The suspect began wailing in agony, as both of his arms flung around wildly in an attempt to wipe the scalding pepper spray from his gash. Now the other officers observed my steel handcuffs dangling from the suspect's left wrist and viewed it as a weapon, as the metal cuff swung back and forth when the suspect attempted to rub his forehead. Two officers repeatedly punched the suspect in the face while shouting, "Stop resisting," causing him to fall down onto the couch. The suspect's girlfriend—who was in the kitchen—ran into the room, began yelling at us, expressing her concern that we were going to physically hurt the suspect further. Once on the sofa, I escorted the suspect's hands behind his back and placed his right wrist in the handcuff without resistance.

When officers use force against citizens I have found, from experience, that the officers use manipulation techniques in order to cast their actions in a better light if viewed by citizens. For example, as I just explained, the majority of officers are prone to shout out phrases that lead a bystander to believe the suspect is resisting, when in all actuality the suspect is struggling to get his hands behind his back but cannot do so with the officer(s) on top of him or her. In addition, officers will delay handcuffing a suspect whom they are arresting so that they may inflict additional physical punishment on the suspect. These actions by the officers can be very detrimental to the relationship between the police and community. For instance, if a citizen actually views the officer's actions as excessive or records the episode on video, then the officers may face termination, being charged criminally, and face public scrutiny. The conduct of these officers severely blemishes the relationship between the police department and the community as a whole. Their disturbing actions, when scrutinized by the public, casts a shadow over the honorable officers who maintain professionalism in the manner which they treat citizens. If these wrong doings are not brought forward by citizens, they are rarely made aware of by officers who were present on scene. This code of silence is ingrained in the minds of young officers, both in the academy and by jaded veteran officers who preach the Us vs. Them mentality.

Furthermore, citizens become upset when they observe police officers not treating members of their community with respect. As explained earlier, some officers routinely walk handcuffed suspects through the middle of the street with their jeans around their ankles. Although it would only take the officer a few seconds to assist the male and pull up his pants, the officer takes it personal that the person ran from him to avoid arrest and attempts to compensate his personal hurt by humiliating the male. Citizens who witness this do not know what the individual ran for; however, after observing the officer degrade the youth in their community, it would not matter to the appalled citizen what crime the youth committed. At that point, the citizens' opinion instantaneously shifts from gratitude toward officers for keeping their neighborhood safe to a belief that the officers are harassing and unfairly targeting individuals in their community. As a result, the citizens are less likely to cooperate with authorities in the future. Furthermore, they will most likely tell numerous friends and relatives what transpired causing a chain reaction of negative publicity and mistrust.

Police officials at the upper level can also sever public relations between the police and the community. When wrongdoings happen in the upper management by the police department, citizen protests usually occur and conspiracy theories arise. It is then up to political figures such as the mayor, chief of police, or city council members to rationalize the incident to the infuriated citizens and entice them to maintain order. For example, I can recall when two officers approached a vehicle leaving a known drug house early in the morning. The suspected vehicle containing two juvenile males had drugs and a handgun inside the vehicle. The driver opened fire on the officers as they approached his vehicle. As the officers returned fire, the driver, for reasons unknown to this day, shot himself in his head instantaneously killing himself. That morning a captain on my department misinformed our public relations lieutenant about what had actually occurred. The lieutenant, believing he had accurate facts, released a press statement that the officers were in reality the ones who shot and killed the driver. Therefore, later when the correct account of the incident was revealed and a new press release was offered, many citizens were convinced that this was the result of a police cover-up. A few weeks later, the county medical examiner concluded an autopsy on the shooter and determined the cause of death to be from a self-inflicted gunshot wound to the head. However, this report did little to appease the citizens who already concluded that police officials were covertly attempting to disguise what had occurred the morning of the tragic shooting. Soon to follow, several hundred protesters marched through the city streets to the police station and concluded their demonstration in front of the city hall. Newspaper editorials were flooded with hatred toward police and the county medical examiner. Officers had taken extra precautions when patrolling the area where the driver killed himself, in fear of being shot at by a sniper. Several years later, citizens still express their displeasure about how the incident was handled and state they will always feel a sense of distrust among police and public officials.

Officers at any level of the department structure can spark animosity toward the police. It is each individual officer's responsibility to not only use the training which the department provides when dealing with individuals in stressful situations, but treat individuals the way you would want a loved one to be treated in any situation. If you allow the citizen's actions to determine how you will handle the call, then the officer can successfully eliminate their personal values and biases and nonjudgmentally treat the citizen. It is crucial to remember that if for every citizen who witnesses an act of misconduct by an officer, that citizen will convey what they witnessed and their displeasure with numerous other citizens. Therefore, good positive police advertising will never outweigh excellent professional police work.

Chapter 3

Police Department Structure Contributing to the Demise of the Inner-city Family

The structure of police departments can play a detrimental part in the collapse of inner-city families. Unscrupulous police officers can go unnoticed, as their behaviors become the norm. Outstanding officers are molded into making questionable decisions from an unethical standpoint as the pressures to conform weighs heavily on them. The comradery among officers and persuasion to conform to this code of behaviors lies within the infrastructure of the department. Soon the department separates itself from the community it swore to protect and takes on a separate identity that cannot relate to its citizens. When examining the framework of a police department, several issues need to be addressed within, to ease the ill feelings between the police and the community they protect.

First, the police department needs to take proactive steps to recruit and retain qualified minority candidates. My department attempted to achieve this by offering a high number of bonus points for applicants who lived within the city. This plan had good intentions due to the fact that a large number of minority individuals resided in the city; however, the strategy did not work for a few reasons. First, the department never made an effort to refute the negative stereotypes regarding officers and the police department as discussed earlier. Second, many of the qualified applicants who originally showed interest were indifferent to take the exam after learning that our department consisted primarily of white male officers. These disproportionate numbers in sex and race among officers could be consistently recognized on any shift. For example, when I was a sergeant on the midnight shift, we had over forty officers on our shift, all but two were white males. Potential African-American applicants would routinely come into the station to ride along with officers in order to determine if they wished to pursue a career in law enforcement. Many of the competent African-American applicants would be distraught after observing the scarce number of minority officers.

The discouragement of minority applicants continues the habitual cycle of an abundance of white male officers within my department. A very discerning problem arises when the majority of these white male recruits come from the suburbs.

The majority of these officers never grew up around minorities, nor are familiar with the subculture within the inner city. For instance, it was not uncommon to work with a white officer from the suburbs who had no African-American friends throughout his childhood. Therefore, with few African-American officers on the police department, the only interaction the officer has with African-Americans occurs on the job with either victims or suspects. Without surprise, based on the officer's limited interactions with African-Americans prior to becoming a police officer, the officer would soon develop negative stereotypes toward members of the race merely based on their numerous encounters with uncooperative African-American victims, and their repeated encounters with defiant African-American suspects. I, on the other hand, grew up with approximately 90 percent of my friends being African-American so I was able to have an objective view and judge each person based on their own individuality.

One example that occurred early on in my career involved a fellow officer who was raised in a predominately white neighboring suburb and he openly voiced his hatred toward the African-American community. One evening, I witnessed his verbal vexation turn physically abusive toward a young African-American male who had eluded the overweight officer on two occasions earlier in the shift. The individual had several warrants out for his arrest and I spotted him in front of a large high-rise apartment complex. The suspect saw my marked police vehicle and attempted to flee on foot; however, I drove over the curb and tree lawn and cut the young male off in the parking lot. The suspect, who was tired from the two prior foot chases with the potbellied officer, immediately surrendered without incident. I secured the individual in handcuffs and began searching the compliant arrested subject with the help of a young strapping officer who arrived on scene to offer assistance. We continued our search of the arrested party and placed his belongings from his pockets on the trunk of a vehicle next to us. The husky officer then arrived on scene, out of breath and extremely flush in the face. He pushed me forcefully on my left shoulder causing me to stumble to my right, away from the arrested individual. The irate officer had his sturdy flashlight in his right hand and began striking the handcuffed prisoner in the head with it. The arrested male yelled for the out-of-control officer to stop as the blows were delivered with such force I could hear a loud bone-chilling smack as each swing of the flashlight struck the defenseless suspect's skull. The officer then began violently swinging the flashlight in an upward motion several times while targeting the pleading prisoner's testicles. After three or four blows, which caused the suspect to crumple over, the irrepressible officer finally showed mercy on the unshielded suspect and ceased his attack. Following the obese officer's onslaught, the once cooperative suspect became enraged from the unprovoked battering and attempted to spit on me as I placed him inside the transport wagon. The suspect—who was livid by how unfairly he was treated and how his rights were violated—began kicking the inside compartment of the wagon to express his displeasure. I recall thinking to myself that if this subversive officer would commit such a heinous injustice against an African-American suspect in front of a well-populated apartment building with numerous potential witnesses, what kind of devious acts would he commit against members of the race in a dimly-lit backyard out of the public eye? Regarding the incident, the well-built officer who came to my aid and I reported the incident to our supervisor. As a result, I broke the unwritten code of silence that is expected between officers and instead of the pudgy officer's actions being condemned by the shift, I was ridiculed by coworkers and labeled as an officer who could not be trusted to cover for officers who use unnecessary force against citizens.

Another drawback to commissioning predominately white suburban officers exists in the form of a communication barrier between the officers and the African-American communities. I found while growing up among many minority families in the inner city that it is accepted to be very expressive when showing feelings of grief or disconcertment. On the other hand, the white culture predominantly conveys this through despondency among each other. When relating this to police work, I observed on a multitude of occasions where an African-American individual would be yelling on a call while expressing his or her point of view and an officer would arrest the individual for disorderly conduct. Officers would consistently use the disorderly conduct charge as a means not to sort out what had transpired before their arrival thus breaking down the communication barrier. The individual had not used obscenities or threatened to hurt someone; however, it was easier for the officer to arrest the person than to deal with a culture the officer was not familiar with. The officer's actions, although easier for him to conduct his job with less hassle, could start a disastrous chain of events for the African-American individual who was only passionately expressing him or herself. As a result, the individual could serve jail time, lose their job, not be able to pay their rent, and be unable to provide for their family. The difference in the way cultures express themselves is one of several ways officers can develop the Us vs. Them way of thinking. If the officer fails to communicate well with individuals in different cultures they are more likely to see the other cultures as inferior, and mistreatment of that group by the officer will consciously or subconsciously be justified to the officer.

Directly out of the police academy young officers are subjected to the internal makeup of the department that sways them to make arrests in order to be accepted by the veteran officers. After graduating from the academy, officers are eager to make big arrests or get into a high-speed car chase to gain attention from their superiors and fellow officers. However, a problem that exists is that new recruits are assigned to the patrol division directly out of the academy. With this assignment, the energetic recruit has insufficient time to follow up and look into major crimes or drug trafficking complaints. High-profile cases such as these are usually investigated by detectives. Therefore, new recruits try to counteract their lack of time given to investigate major cases by stopping countless cars in predominately minority dominated neighborhoods in an attempt to recover drugs or a gun in the car. In addition, the driver of the vehicle may have a felony warrant for his arrest or may decide to flee on foot, or in his vehicle from the police.

The new officer's yearning for acceptance starts a cycle that debilitates young minorities in crime-ridden areas who are obeying society's laws. I have seen it as a common practice that new officers habitually make traffic stops on young minorities for very minor infractions. These traffic stops which occur although justified according to state law—such as the vehicle's rear license plate light was burned out—but they are actually initiated because the officer is looking to see if the occupants have warrants, drugs, or a weapon. If the officer is satisfied that nothing illegal has taken place and the driver is respectful toward his authority, then the driver is traditionally released with a warning. The start of the cycle that is ruinous to the inner-city family occurs when this experience is repeated numerous times by officers to the law-abiding minority.

I would frequently ask this next generation of African-American males how many times they had been stopped in the past year. The majority of the young minority drivers would have to answer the question in terms of being stopped in a month because traffic stops involving them was so habitual. The general consensus of the individual who shared their encounters with me had experienced between six to eight traffic stops a month. I would frequently examine these young minorities' criminal record and routinely found that they had little or no criminal record other than minor traffic violations. The most common charge on their criminal record was for disorderly conduct. I wondered how these youths had so many traffic violations but few criminal charges against them. My pondering was short lived as I began letting other officers drive more often, leaving me more time to observe and digest my partner's interaction with members of the community. I quickly began to see the young minorities again, who had few criminal arrest records, from the multitude of traffic stops my partner was conducting. The young minorities eventually had attitudes after they were pulled over and they routinely questioned my partner's reason for the traffic stop. From that point, the hostility between the driver and my partner usually grew throughout the stop. The standoff between the two generally ended in the driver receiving as many traffic citations as my partner could give him. Furthermore, I oftentimes saw the communication collapse into a shouting match between the two parties. This would routinely lead to the driver being arrested for disorderly conduct. At first hand, I witnessed how the cycle swirled into a chaos that left young minorities feeling violated and infuriated at the police. I could not blame how they were feeling and I would be hypocritical if I said they had no right. Likewise, I was sure I would undergo the same emotions if my family member or I were stopped six to eight times a month by police officers for minor violations. In comparison, I wholeheartedly knew that in the predominately white areas, officers rarely made traffic stops on the individuals who lived in the prosperous communities.

In relation, the minority youth, who was originally cooperative and respectful toward the police, grew more flustered with each traffic stop and began to express his or her displeasure toward his or her dealings with the police. The officer would most likely see this as a challenge to his authority that would lead to an argument and oftentimes the driver would be arrested for disorderly conduct. I would become appalled in these circumstances that the officer could not take him or herself out of the current situation and examine the entire chain of events which took a cooperative unworldly African-American youth and swiftly made him into a disheartened individual, which led to the breakdown in communication.

Another factor tied into the political realm on a police department is the immense pressure for totals. Totals are the statistical amount of work an officer can be measured by during a time period. To illustrate, one officer could have 125 traffic citations and thirty-two criminal arrests in a given month. Meanwhile, another officer could have eighty-six traffic citations and twelve criminal arrests in a month. Problems arise when police departments put too much emphasis merely on the statistical data instead of the quality of work. For example, if a person were to examine the figures above, most people would assume that the first police officer was a more diligent worker than the second. However, in all actuality the second officer may work a slower shift, may follow up more on previous calls, may have made more serious arrests which took him off the street for long periods of time to complete paperwork, or recently took time off work.

In relation, if departments only focus on statistical numbers then officers will compete for recognition through statistical data. This proved true in my police department when they posted the number of each officer's arrests, parking tickets, and traffic citations on an office wall each month. This type of policing can be detrimental to the public because many officers stopped doing other aspects of police work such as community policing that was not a category on the monthly evaluation sheets. Furthermore, and probably the most unfair to the citizens, officers would issue traffic citations or make arrests under conditions where they normally would give the person a warning. The stress officers had from the city to conform were enormous when you figured in that a portion of the city revenue depended on the fines from arrests and citations. However, the methodology used was an insufficient determinant to measure how competently an officer did his or her job. My department—which used a number system—was similar to the Ohio State Patrol, which has adopted a point system. However, the purpose of generating cash revenue by pressuring police actions appears to have a deep rooted correlation between the politician's attempt to term their program, hoping to gain public support.

A gigantic problem that can affect citizens in a prejudicial way is the manner in which officers are paid for going to court. My department, like many others, pays the officers a flat rate of four hours for their appearance in court so long as the case is less than four hours in length. Several dilemmas occur under this system, which indirectly affect the citizens and their quality of life. First, the officers get paid for four hours; however, I found through my almost fifteen years and hundreds of court cases that the average time spent in court was approximately twenty minutes. In the vast majority of the cases, the defendant would enter a plea to a lesser charge and the officer would be on his or her way. I frequently observed that once young officers found out that they could get paid four additional hours pay for twenty minutes of work, an overwhelming number of officers would vacate their discretion and morals in order to arrest and issue citations to a multitude of citizens. These actions were not done with the oath to serve and protect in mind, but the mere hope of receiving court cases for monetary gain. To make matters worse, I habitually observed numerous officers start to budget their court cases into their living expenses. This formula proved disastrous for citizens who came into contact with these court-seeking officers, because the officer would not take into account the public or citizen's best interest but instead the interest of his or her financial lifestyle. As a result, the citizen is less likely to get a break from the officer, causing a downhill spiral of unjust strife for the citizen and his or her family, as court fines and jail time become a reality based on the officer's alternative motive.

Another defective aspect within the police department comes when subdivision jobs are awarded as part of an exempt interview process instead of by seniority. To illustrate, my department awards its narcotics unit positions using the exempt method. This reward system negatively affects its citizens in numerous ways. For example, throughout my career I witnessed officers conduct countless illegal searches on citizens, houses, and vehicles in an attempt to recover drugs. These unlawful searches were conducted in hopes of gaining the attention of narcotic supervisors to further their endeavor of working for the unit. Meanwhile, the citizen had his or her civil rights violated at the expense of the officer's attempt to further his career. Therefore, the violated citizen will convey his or her displeasure regarding their encounter with the police at block watches, to friends and family, to community leaders, and oppose any future police levies, all because of one unscrupulous officer.

Hiring through exemption also causes the officer to focus exclusively on the particular field they are trying to be assigned. For example, I observed many officers who desperately wanted to be assigned to the street narcotics unit. As a result, they focused an absorbent amount of their police time stopping suspected drug dealers. Now don't get me wrong, I wanted drug dealers off the street also and made numerous drug arrests throughout my career; however, several officers who aspired to go to the street narcotics unit would frequently undermine other calls in order to focus on making drug arrests. There were several incidents where a female was clearly victimized by her lover and a domestic violence arrest was warranted; however, the officer would just refer the victim to the prosecutors' officer or give the suspect a ride away from the residence. On one such occasion, a female frantically flagged my partner and I down to report that her husband had assaulted her. The distraught female had a swollen upper lip and nose. In addition, strands of her hair were stuck together by blood which seeped from her head. My partner asked the victim if the assailant was home. The trembling female informed us that her husband had fled the scene. My partner, who was on the way to check on a drug house before being stopped by the distressed victim, advised the injured party to return home and call the police back if her husband returned. As a result of the officer's tunnel vision and personal agenda to receive the exempt position, citizens' safety was put in jeopardy and other unrelated crimes not pertaining to drugs went uninvestigated.

These repeated acts of violating the citizens' liberties by police officers causes a breakdown in the union between public and police; however, the coalition is needed to work together in order to solve crimes and keep neighborhoods protected. The parting of the union can be a direct result of a city having an abundance of unsolved homicides. As a result of the parting, citizens feel less of a responsibility to get involved and come forward if they have information or have witnessed a horrific crime. The separation results in mutual feelings of distrust and hatred between citizens and officers. To illustrate how infuriated citizens are with the police, violent video games such as Grand Theft Auto—which depict street thugs vividly murdering officers—are flying off the shelves in astronomical numbers. In addition, street rappers seem to rely on songs about executing police officers as the way to build their credibility in both the music industry and on the street. In the future, these young game players and aspiring rappers will have a distorted image of the police and will be less willing to mend any past dilemmas that strain relations. If they continue to live in a subculture that promotes executing innocent officers, then the morals of these individuals will change and their detachment toward officers and rebelliousness toward authority figures will widen. Therefore, officers must be able to adequately communicate with inner-city families; however, an enormous barrier was present at my department when dealing with non-English speaking families. For instance, my department did not offer any form of training for officers to learn to speak another language. With a growing Hispanic population, this valuable training could save an officer's or citizen's life in a stressful situation. For example, if an officer was sufficiently trained to speak Spanish and responded to a call regarding a Spanish-speaking suspect waving a gun in the air, the officer would be able to order the individual to drop the gun in Spanish. As a result, the officer's successful communication could enable the scenario to be resolved peacefully. In addition, officers would be able to communicate with victims on domestic violence calls and gain a full understanding of the amount of abuse the victim was enduring to sufficiently gather information for an arrest and successful prosecution. Unfortunately, my department takes a reactive stance on providing training in this area, which will inevitably result in the demise of an officer, death, or continued abuse of a non-English-speaking citizen due to the contributing factor of the lack of communication before proper training is given.

The lower level workforce in the police hierarchy, such as the officers and sergeants, has the most interaction with the citizens. In my experience, I have become assimilated to the fact that use of force investigations by the sergeant who investigates an officer(s)' physical actions against a citizen(s) was tainted by the informal proceedings, which took place immediately following the use of force. To illustrate, it became unwritten common practice for the investigating sergeant to interview the citizen and any witnesses first regarding what had transpired between he or she and the police officer(s). The sergeant would then double-cross the citizen and witnesses and divulge their statement to the officer(s) involved. This unethical practice would allow the officer(s) to devise their written report to refute any excessive use of force allegations by the citizen and witnesses. If the investigation were conducted properly, first, the officers would not be allowed to talk to each other and would have to write separate reports. It is by departmental procedure to separate multiple suspects in a crime when reasonably possible, and have them separately interviewed; yet we do not require our officers to be dutiful by completing the same process. As a result, incidents where officers use an unjust amount of force to subdue a citizen is likely to go unproven. This will leave the combative officer still on the street and the citizens affected from the incident both dejected and agitated with the criminal justice system.

Chapter 4

Unaccounted for Police Strains

In order for officers to successfully treat citizens' calls for help with compassion, the officer must be free of personal distractions which may affect his or her judgment. Obstacles which present themselves in the officer's personal life such as divorce or the death of a loved one can lead to the officer detaching him or herself from the citizens' needs. I routinely witnessed officers going to work under heartbreaking conditions after immediately suffering a loss. The officer would typically handle his or her call with the least amount of effort possible. Therefore, citizens would feel slighted by the service they received, which caused many individuals whom the officer encountered to believe that all officers would show little concern about their dilemma. I frequently would attempt to convince the struggling officer to take some personal days off in order to reinvigorate him or herself. However, most attempts were strongly opposed because the majority of the officers felt that the time off would only give him or her more unfruitful time to ponder their loss. As a result, the disengaged officer would work a high-stressed demanding job, while placing themselves, their partner, and citizens at risk to be hurt or killed due to their apathetic work ethic. The feeling of hopelessness an officer feels when he or she attempts to deal with grief can be a much harder obstacle to overcome than a citizen who is experiencing a similar loss. This occurs because officers are usually alienated from society in such a way that the officer is the one who has to solve or make the correct referrals to aid in the citizens' recovery, not the other way around. In addition, because police departments are predominately men, these subcultures take on an egotistical "macho" mentality, which causes officers to suppress their anxiety and fears within themselves. I have found through my experience that when officers suppress feelings, it plays a part in the officer alienating him or her from family, friends, and their workplace, which can lead to suicide, alcoholism, divorce, or illicit drug use.

When examining the divorce rates among police officers, it is disheartening to know that 60 to 75 percent of all marriages involving a police officer ends in a divorce. This statistic is substantially higher than the 50 percent of all civilians whose marriages end in divorce (Heavy Badge 2010). These statistics, and for the officers who lived through a divorce, can prove very demoralizing when the officer repeatedly attempts to mend domestic issues involving citizens, when in all actuality it is statistically harder for officers to restore their own faltering marriage. I have personal knowledge that problems usually first fester within the officer and then eventually reveal themselves outwardly, causing a deterioration of the officer's work and family life. To illustrate, when my own marriage became in a state of dishevelment, I would continuously arrive on calls and would stand unconcerned about the citizen or solving their problem. For example, an elderly female telephoned police and summoned me about a neighbor who had sideswiped her vehicle while backing out of their shared driveway. I can vividly recall standing there with a blank stare as the gray-haired lady complained and in my mind I was screaming, "Lady, who thinks you have problems! I am going through a divorce and losing my first love." After about a month of playing my favorite gospel CDs, reading self-help books, and thumbing through the Bible, I knew I could not overcome my feelings of helplessness on my own. Furthermore, I was convinced if I continued to work in my present state of mind, citizens would not be receiving the best service I knew I could provide, and officers including myself would be at risk to be hurt due to my inattentiveness.

Although I realized that I needed counseling to help me cope with my divorce, for weeks I resisted my conscience's own pleas to take the next steps and seek treatment. After wrestling with the advantages and disadvantages of how a psychologist would be perceived and affect my masculinity, I sheepishly went to the department's Employee Assistance program, located across the street from the police station. I made sure to walk there when the least number of officers would be walking to their cruiser to report for duty. In addition, I wore a black New York Yankees cap with the brim pulled down to my eyebrows. Although I took several precautions not to be recognized, to my dismay after entering the building, I learned that the Employee Assistance program was disbanded due to city budget cuts.

It took me a lot of courage that day to first, admit that I needed help, and second, seek the service of a qualified psychologist. However, after that day I never built up enough undaunted feelings to get professional help until two years later. During those two years, I held in anger, regrets, and unresolved psychological hurts. I was reluctant to seek an alleviation from my distress because I knew how inhumane the subculture within the department acts. For instance, on one occasion, a fellow officer told his supervisor about a particular wrongdoing a few officers did to a civilian. A few days later, the officer who was attempting to protect the rights of the citizen received a tampon inside of his police mailbox. Therefore, I cowardly feared more about what other officers would think and say about me getting help than I did about my own personal healing and myself.

Another complication police departments have is when is it the department's obligation to intervene if an officer is excessively consuming alcoholic beverages if he or she is drinking off duty? My department had no alcohol outreach program for an officer to turn to when struggling with alcoholism. We did have a police chaplain; however, he was not a specialist in the field. With no professional support within the department, officers would continue to indulge in alcohol. I routinely saw these officers drinking heavily at police functions such as union meetings, fundraisers, or whatever else they could think of to give them a flimsy excuse to drink. Like clockwork the next day, the officer would drag themselves into work feeling irritable and devitalized. This was the everyday habit among most alcoholics on my department. The drawback to this environment is that my department did not proactively seek out officers whose consumption of alcohol had become unmanageable, nor did they have a program set up where the officer could go to for assistance. It was a well-known fact among city officials and police supervisors that alcohol abuse involving police officers is estimated to be double the United States' general population of one in ten adults (Violanti 1999).

Problems off duty may occur as a result of my department taking a reactive approach when dealing with officers' drinking problems. These include a tragedy such as a traffic fatality, a domestic violence quarrel, or spiral into the officer going through a depression state and taking his or her own life. For example, one officer who was briefly my partner at one point in my career was inordinately consuming alcohol for a man of his 5'7" stature at a nightclub with several other officers. When the officer left the club he joked about how he was going to go home and "beat" his "old lady." The inebriated officer drove himself home, a short distance away, to the wife of his children. Shortly after arriving at his residence, the police were summoned to respond to a domestic dispute. After arriving on scene, the officers located the intoxicated officer's wife hiding scarcely clothed in the bushes. Following an investigation, the officer was arrested for domestic violence and spent well over a year negotiating to regain employment.

By taking a reactive approach, problems as the one described can only be dealt with after they occur. As a result, the victim already has undergone the traumatic incident and the officer has to face the consequences of his or her actions. In the incident described, several other officers and myself were highly aware of the officer's overindulgent drinking habits. However, we did not intervene to help the officer mainly because the subculture of the police department uses alcohol consumption as a way to decompress among fellow officers, and there was not a program set up at the station to direct him where the officer could receive counseling for alcoholism. As pointed out earlier, our Employee Assistance program was cut due to funding, our health insurance allows an officer to seek help at a private psychological facility, and Alcoholics Anonymous is always an option. However, after being lied to by so many criminals, officers become jaded and begin to only trust their families or other officers. This feeling of skepticism can be ill-fated if their police department does not have an alcohol counselor on staff, or there is not an officer advocate who can refer and support the alcoholic officer.

When officers struggle with alcoholism, the officer's family and the community which he or she serve suffers as well. For instance, I frequently observed officers, while working, sleep in their cruisers after a night of heavy drinking. At first thought, the average citizen would become upset because their tax dollars were being wasted on a sleeping officer. However, if you look deeper into the issue, if the officer would not have been drinking and would have been alert and doing what he or she took the oath to do, then the officer may put him or herself in a position to stop or prevent a crime such as a rape. So in actuality the officer's alcohol problem can contribute to major crimes occurring and innocent citizens being traumatized by these horrendous crimes. In addition, officers who report to work ailing from the previous night of drinking are likely to treat the citizens without due regard. Therefore if the officer is incorrigible, the citizen's disgruntlement will lead to the citizen filing a formal complaint against the officer, the citizen voting against future police levies, and publicly speaking out regarding their dissatisfaction with the police. These are additional circumstances which support the much-needed proactive intervention to address alcoholism at the police level.

On a brisk January morning in 2005, I responded to a call that later took me to the brink of alcoholism which plagued my father and grandfather throughout their adult lives. Another officer and I were dispatched to respond to an industrial accident involving a teenage male. The company had its workers use its machines to shred and bale wasted paper. My teeth clinched together when I read the call notes on my cruiser's computer, which informed me that a teenager was trapped inside a baler machine. After arriving on scene shortly after EMS, I observed what I believed to be two individuals inside of the machine, because I could see an individual's head facing me and another person's feet resting on top of the first individual's head. However, after getting within reach of the baler I was horrified to find out that there was only the teenage male inside of the apparatus. My stomach grew nauseous as I could graphically see that the powerful steel baler had slammed the youth's defenseless body, along with shredded paper underneath the machine and into a half bale of shredded paper. The heels of the young man's feet were touching the back of his own head from being compressed by the contraption, giving an illusion from a distance that two people were inside of the machine. The EMS staff scrambled to rifle through the slivers of paper in a desperate attempt to rescue the trapped youth who was clinging to life. When EMS finally got to the teenager, I was overcome with an eerie feeling, which I had never experienced on a call before. I can recall when EMS pulled the youth out of the machine, that the only thing keeping his upper body connected to his lower body at the pelvic region was the skin on his back. EMS rapidly placed the teenage on a stretcher, causing the youth to wail in excruciating pain with every movement of his crumpled body. I distinctly remember at one point when he was finally loaded into the EMS unit, where he was face down on the gurney but his feet were positioned pointing upward. Despite the grim circumstances, I was approached by a shaken young male—who would turn out to be the incapacitated male's brother—who handed me a rosary to place in the EMS unit with his sibling. I fulfilled his brother's wish and transported the distraught brother to the hospital behind the EMS unit. On the way to the hospital I inquired as to how the tragic accident occurred. The shocked young man told me that he and his brother worked at another company; however, they were making some extra money on a Saturday morning by modifying the baler machine. He continued to explain that a manager of the company advised them that the machine was turned off and they were given approval to work on the contraption. However, in all actuality the machine was not turned off but set to automatically bale when the infrared eye detects that it is full. So when his brother entered the machine, the eye sensed that it was full and baled the youth. Shortly before arriving at the hospital, I was burdened with the heavy-hearted task of calling the youth's parents and informing them of the tragedy. The youth's father seemed to be in a state of disbelief as I explained to him without any graphic details that his son was involved in an industrial accident and his injuries were substantial. I further informed him that he would be needed at the hospital. The mother, who was at a separate location, expressed her distraught more openly so I sent an officer to her residence to arrange for her to come to the hospital.

After dropping the sibling off at the hospital, I remember pulling into an empty school parking lot and uncontrollably crying. I was disturbed by the fact that it was Saturday morning, and most youths their age would be home sleeping off a hangover; but these two young men were attempting to make an honest pay by helping out another company, and disaster struck. How fair is that? I repeatedly thought to myself. These are good kids I thought over and over to myself. Why did one have to physically be subjected to the machine's unforgiving power while his brother helplessly watched? To top it off, the sibling was carrying a piece of his faith in the form of a rosary. These feelings ran through my mind countless times over the next two months and it made me question my faith, because I could not view what happened as being fair.

Throughout the next few months, I drank beer every evening until I was well beyond intoxicated and my mind would no longer attempt to decipher the justification of what had occurred. I learned that the young man had lived; however, he no longer had the lower half of his body below his belly button. I rarely drank alcohol beverages, but this was a way to prevent me from personalizing the obstacles ahead for the young man, and temporarily stop my search for an answer to why this occurred. Every morning I came into work hung over and sluggishly answered my dispatched calls while not conducting any proactive work. I thought about seeing a psychologist, but I was afraid that if someone from work found out, I would be labeled a cowardly officer. It took me approximately sixty days until I finally started viewing the incident as a miracle rather than a tragedy. Here is a youth who by the grace of God is still alive to touch, feel, and love. After I started to view that he lived as a blessing, I stopped my binge consumption of beer and started once again working at a skillful level. During my dismay, citizens did not receive the proper police support they needed from me. As a result of one family's tragedy, I failed to immediately seek professional help and this error probably contributed to the downfall of several other families; I could have helped resolve their differences if I was working with a clear and sober mind.

Another undisclosed predicament officers place themselves in which will evidently harm the citizens and their own personal health is the use of steroids in police work. From my experience using the drug, and from watching several other officers' use, we would justify the utilization of steroids as a tool of the trade. I knew that anabolic steroids made me physically bigger, faster, and stronger which is what I needed to have in order to catch the younger in-shape criminals. I first began using anabolic steroids shortly after the mentally-ill individual unsnapped my holster and took my handgun halfway out of the holster. After that incident, I became aware that just because I wore a badge and carried a gun, I was not invincible. I was quickly aging, working alone, and the majority of the criminals I was frequently encountering were almost half my age. For several nights after the incident I had nightmares; however, during each of the bad dreams the mentally-ill person actually took my handgun from me and I was repeatedly begging for my life. I was puzzled about what to do because I already possessed a department-issued handgun for protection, yet that appeared to be not enough. The police subculture subconsciously put enormous pressure on me not to seek professional counseling in fear of looking weak and incompetent. For the next few weeks, I pondered how I could protect myself and what I should do about my insecurity. Finally, I remembered my late teenage years at the neighborhood gym. I recalled the muscular guys at the gym bench-pressing so much weight that the steel bar would slightly bend as they pushed the weight off their strapping pectorals. This memory enlivened me, as I believed the remedy for all my insecurities regarding my increasing age, working alone, and being overpowered would be solved in a bottle of anabolic steroids.

That evening, I contacted an old acquaintance from the gym and inquired about purchasing anabolic steroids from him. The individual was at first very suspicious of my desire to purchase the drug because of my position as a police officer. However after much convincing, the individual agreed to sell me a 10 ml. bottle of testosterone. The acquaintance showed me how to draw up the testosterone from the vial and where to inject the oily narcotic. He placed me on a workout regime and high protein diet during the six-week cycle of taking the steroid. After the six weeks, I was hooked from the immense gains I made from the program. In addition to the twenty pounds of muscle I gained while actually becoming leaner, I also acquired a commanding presence and self-confidence which overshadowed any insecurity. My muscular frame and newly-found zeal was allowing me to work longer hours, handle calls by myself without worries, and arrest dicey criminals without difficulty.

For almost the next decade as a police officer, I used anabolic steroids on and off, depending on how confident I felt in handling calls involving well-built offenders. Through the years, I consistently worked out at our gym inside of the police station. There were numerous episodes during that time period when officers would compliment me on my physique. The compliment was usually followed up with an inquiry if I was using steroids. I always adamantly denied using steroids because I never knew if the officer could be completely trusted and was not working for internal affairs. I would only be honest with the officer if they shared with me first that they were on steroids or if they desired to take them. During the times I used steroids, I obtained steroids for four other officers who wanted the narcotic, three of which were later repeat buyers. After using steroids for so long and becoming part of the underground culture it presents, I could usually tell who was using steroids by things such as the fullness in their face, mannerism, acne, and extreme gains in weight and strength. Therefore, although I knew myself and four other officers were using steroids for sure, I suspected numerous other officers who had used throughout the years I indulged. At the time, I did not see my actions or the other officers' actions as wrong. I perceived our acts as an effort to better enhance ourselves physically, which allowed us to more advantageously defend ourselves and the citizens.

In June of 2010, two of the four officers that I was getting steroids for and I were arrested by our own department for steroid possession and possessing syringes. This was undoubtedly the most embarrassing and shameful experience of my life. I had just finished my college degree in nursing three weeks prior, and had aspirations to leave the police department to pursue medical mission work. Now I was on the front page of the local newspaper for my lawlessness. I always believed that my actions were permissible based on the dangerous line of work I was in and the fact that I was nearly murdered with my own weapon. However, it was not until I was forced to attend over twenty three-hour intensive outpatient group therapy sessions, that I was diagnosed with post-traumatic stress disorder relating to the incident where my gun was almost taken from me by the mentally-ill individual. It was then that I realized that the steroid use was attempts to self-medicate myself and to give me energy and make me feel more secure. Through several emotional counseling sessions, I worked conscientiously with the psychologist to regain a lot of my feelings of insecurities I lost on that dreadful day.

After completing numerous therapy sessions for my post-traumatic stress disorder, I came face to face with the heartrending realization that there are probably thousands of officers in the United States currently patrolling the streets who have this disorder but either were afraid to come forward for treatment, or do not realize they have it. Officers live in a world where seeing burned bodies, raped children, and severely abused elderly people are the norm. Yet they also survive in a police subculture that scrutinizes you and labels you a coward if you show emotions or seek psychological treatment regarding the vivid horrors you see. I am displeased that it took me getting arrested to fully comprehend the psychological effect that the job had on me. However, the end result was worth it because I was able to begin to truly cope with my disorder and educate other officers about the importance of expressing oneself and seeking professional help when needed. As a result, officers will less likely turn to steroids or other drugs to mask their insecurities or suppress their unsettling emotions. This will allow the officers to stand up to the informal intimidations of the police subculture in a more realistic state of mind than under the influence of any drug not prescribed.

The majority of inner-city cops are faced with the actuality of seeing trauma involving infants being molested or shaken to death in a fit of rage by an inadequate caretaker, innocent bystanders being murdered from a gang-related drive-by shooting, and elderly citizens being raped and burned to death in an attempt by the perpetrator to conceal evidence. Although officers investigate numbers of these types of atrocious incidents throughout his or her career, it only takes one of these types of calls to leave the officer feeling hopeless and despondent. Once the officer accepts unjust responsibility for the crime he or she is investigating, and not seek professional counseling, the officer may develop post-traumatic stress disorder which if untreated can be detrimental to the officer. An officer may feel a sense of discouragement when he or she is obtaining evidence and confessions necessary to prosecute a case against a child molester; meanwhile, numerous other reprehensible crimes against several other children are compiling in substantial numbers for the officer to also investigate. As a result, I have heard officers complain and tend to agree, that we are not sincerely making a big enough difference, because to effectively piece together, solve, and prosecute a horrid crime it takes an inordinate amount of time put in by the officers, detectives, and prosecutor(s) in charge of the case. In comparison, for the hundreds of hours necessary to investigate, apprehend, and successfully prosecute a child molester, it is easy for a detective to get behind and feel submerged in his work; because it only takes a few seconds of an unworldly child being alone with a deplorable person to commit an inexcusable sexual act on the child, resulting in another innocent person being abused and the extensive investigative process starting again. Therefore, by the time a detective does his or her part in successfully placing the culprit in jail, numerous other loathsome incidents have occurred during the time of the detective's involvement in the last victorious prosecution, leaving an abundant amount of new cases to investigate. As a result, the caseload becomes overbearing and the pressure to both catch up and solve the crimes can become unmanageable. The detective is quickly faced with the political pressures from his or her supervisors, possible media inquiry, the victim, and the victim's family wanting to know about the case and what progress is being made as the detective struggles not to fall further behind in his or her workload.

During my brief time in the detective bureau, I learned that the better you are as a detective, the more work you generated for yourself, therefore, the further you get behind on your other cases. For example, if you were diligent and questioned suspects thoroughly, the suspects were likely to give you information on other serious crimes that they were not involved in to deflect the current investigation away from themselves. As a result, the good detective would investigate these leads as well, in order to solve additional crimes, resulting in incoming cases not being quickly attended to. As a result, I found that there was a great disparity between detectives who tenaciously work their caseloads and detectives who are lackadaisical in their investigations. Therefore, I urge police departments to promote vigilant supervisors who care that detectives receive equitable workloads, which will ensure that each victim's case will receive a genuine investigation. For example, my department's detective bureau mostly operates by assigning detectives to a particular district and the detective is only in charge of investigating specific crimes committed in that particular district. This method of investigation has repeatedly proved tremendously inconsistent and skewed, because the effort of solving the crime is based on the ambition of the particular detective assigned to the area where the crime occurred. For example, if a burglary was committed in District 3 and the detective assigned to the area was very motivated and enthusiastic about his work, then he or she would conduct a thorough investigation into the crime. This would involve an abundant amount to time, and would also serve as moral compensation to the victim even if the criminal was not arrested. By conducting this extensive probe, the detective is highly likely to develop information which may lead to the future arrest of the perpetrator. On the other hand, if a detective who is assigned to District 3 is lax and whose motives are absent from police work, consequently the detective is likely to put forth little effort into the investigation. The detective's lack of initiative and drive will not likely develop any valuable information to solve the crime. Therefore, this detective treats the victim and the seriousness of the crime to the victim and society in an unjust manner. As a supervisor, you must realize and take into consideration the motives and devotion the detectives who work under you have for their community. I find, from the example provided, that it is more advantageous for the citizens and victim if cases are assigned individually among detectives, instead of by district. As a result, the supervisor is able to see that each case is being exhaustively investigated, and if a detective is investigating a case that is snowballing into a case with multiple other crimes and suspects, then the supervisor can deflect new cases to other detectives while the detective is handling the expanding case.

Detectives and officers encounter enormous departmental and societal tensions when handling high-profile cases in which children are victimized. Pressures from the police department supervisors usually come in the form of constantly pestering the detective assigned to the case, in an attempt to get them to solve the crime and make an arrest. Although citizens and public leaders routinely voice their concerns for the victim and the victim's family following a horrific crime which a child was the victim, the detective and officers who observed the child's morbid state of death are the ones who are personally attached to the crime by vividly realizing that the victim could have been their own daughter, son, niece, or nephew. By seeing the graphic circumstances of the innocent child's death, the detective and officers are able to personalize the death and will likely investigate the crime wholeheartedly. Regularly in these cases, the detectives and officers involved would meticulously rework the crime and crime scene while at work, only to go home and tirelessly reanalyze the context in their mind. The painstaking reality of the law enforcement world is that even if there is a breakthrough in the case and the crime is solved, it is sure that another case will follow. As a result, officers and detectives will be involved in abundance of grisly murder investigations and child rapes throughout their careers; of which, some they will take personal in their pursuit to find the killer(s) or perpetrator(s). My concern comes in the incidences where the killer(s) or perpetrator(s) is not found, how will the officer or detective who investigated the gruesome crime personally react? As explained earlier, it is extremely difficult for officers within the police subculture to express to their coworkers when they felt a citizen's rights were being violated. Therefore, it would be tremendously uncomfortable for an officer or detective to express to his or her coworkers any insecurities, fears of death, or feelings toward a child's vivid victimization they may have.

With no one to confide in, the officer or detective is likely to keep the detailed memories of death and despair deep inside him or her. The person is less likely to seek out professional counseling because, once again, the unforgiving police subculture will likely ridicule and not support the grieving officer. As the sorrow and resentment builds within the officer or detective, the unresolved issues will manifest and develop into an unrealistic sense of sadness and feelings of self-doubt from the withheld emotions. As a result, the officer can develop post-traumatic stress disorder (PTSD), resulting from the unsettled feelings the officer contains within him or herself from the horrendous occurrence. If still untreated, the officer's grief could further spiral to thoughts of, or the act of suicide.

An unfortunate occurrence occurred within my department, which involved a captivating officer who was relatively new to the department, with only a few years experience. Despite his lack of time on the street, the officer seemed to have a charisma to his personality that enabled him to control hostile situations as well as any savvy veteran officer. I found him to be a delight when he showed up on my calls because he would always have a pleasant grin on his face, and a comforting word to say to a victim undergoing a hardship. However, one day the spry officer failed to show up for work, and his supervisors sent a few of his fellow officers out to his residence, to investigate the matter after several phone calls went unanswered. After arriving at the residence, the officers did not receive an answer when they knocked at the door; however, the officers found the back door to be unlocked and entered the residence. Once inside, the officers found the young officer deceased inside of his bathtub from one self-inflicted gunshot wound to his head. The officers who were on the scene were all close-knit friends to the departed officer, and had unexpectedly observed their fellow comrade in a harrowing state. Following the officer's suicide, the officers on scene were given the next day off and required to attend one debriefing session. I found it disgraceful to the tightly-bonded officers, their families, and the citizens they protect, to have required the officers to report back to duty without undergoing extensive professional counseling. In reality, these officers had just unexpectedly observed a horrifying scene involving their coworker and dear friend; the officers were probably just sorting through their feelings when they were instructed to return back to work. Therefore, if the officers suffered from PTSD relating to the tragedy, then the untreated emotions could possibly indirectly come out in a negative or abusive manner in the officers' personal lives or later while working with citizens. It is estimated that 10 percent of all officers fit the criteria for post-traumatic stress disorder; sadly many more go undiagnosed and can become a liability while working the streets (The Badge of Life 2009).

When I ask citizens to visualize how an officer would die, the majority of citizens state that they picture the officer dying in a shootout with a vicious criminal. One individual stated that he envisioned an officer shooting and killing a few masked bank robbers before being shot and killed by a third masked man who possessed a much more high-powered gun than the officer. Astonishingly, what citizens fail to realize is the fact that according to policesuicideprevention.com statistics, 143 officers committed suicide in 2009, compared to 127 officers who died in the line of duty (The Badge of Life 2009). The line of duty fatalities included gunshot wounds, automobile accidents, training exercises, and other unaccounted for occurrences (The Officer Down Memorial Page Inc. 2009). As a result, officers who are overburdened by work or by the emotional impact of repeatedly dealing with death, torment, and other exploitations of the job need to seek professional help outside of the police subculture to help their personal relationships and sanity. By both seeking and obtaining professional counseling, the officer and his or her family will have more resources available to them to overcome many psychological hindrances which may arise from the officer's demanding job. In addition, police departments must take an active role in identifying these officers with post-traumatic stress disorder and require the troubled officers to undergo intensive inpatient or outpatient psychological therapy. Police departments must also take proactive steps to limit the number of traumatic experiences officers endure. One way this can be accomplished is by rotating officers out of the patrol division to other units within the department such as the warrants division or the street narcotics unit. Unfortunately, my department did not practice this creative way to alleviate officers' stress, which manifests with the multitude of gory deaths or severe beatings they routinely see on a day-to-day basis. My department was strictly run on seniority; therefore, many defeated officers spent over fifteen years in the patrol division before they could bid into a specialty unit. By this time, the odds are that severe psychological damage has already been done. The chances that officers suffering from PTSD, or being cynical from their melancholy-filled days in patrol has already taken its toll. As discussed earlier, the psychological stressors may cause the officer to succumb to divorce, alcoholism, or suicide. The rates among police officers are drastically higher compared to the general population. Hopefully, departments can identify the officer's disorder and psychological counseling can help restore the officer's vision of work and repair his or her dispirited family life.

A common fact frequently overlooked by public officials and citizens is that police officers also have families, and if the proper counseling programs are not in place for them when it is their time to seek help, instead of actually giving it, then the officer will have to turn to an unempathizing police subculture. Therefore, it is important that city officials take the steps necessary of ensuring that competent psychologists and psychiatrists are available for police officers when trouble arises in their life. These resources are vital in ensuring that the already high divorce, alcoholism, and suicide rates among police officers do not escalate further. With support from city officials, police supervision, and the professional resources presented, it is viable to believe that the police subculture could change and become more sensitive toward officers' interpersonal needs. As a result, hopefully with time, officers' divorce, alcoholism, and suicide rates will drastically drop. For it is the officers themselves who are the first responders and called out to the scene when inner-city families are in strife, and the officers are tasked with the responsibility to help mend these families. Therefore, officers need to have mended their own families to in-turn protect the demise of another.

Chapter 5

Internal Family Destruction

Police officers are required to enforce detrimental crimes that rip families apart such as murder. However, when officers commit these ghastly acts, it disintegrates the family and usually gains an enormous amount of media attention, forcing the remaining family members to repeatedly relive the incident through distressing news reports and interviews. In addition, the community can lose faith in the police, thus becoming hesitant to work with officers in solving crimes unless it directly affects them. There were two horrific incidents I can recall during my career where a police captain from my department and a patrolman from a neighboring city brutally killed their children's mother. The gruesome murders left their impressionable children without a maternal parent to raise them. As a result, the children's family structure was instantly altered, leaving them behind to attempt to psychologically adjust to the unwelcomed change.

Douglas Prade was a police captain on my department when I came on in 1995. I frequently had police-related conversations with him since we were both assigned to the patrol division. My encounters with him were always pleasant, giving me no insight of what was to come. In April of 1997, Captain Prade and his wife, Dr. Margo Prade, divorced after seventeen years of marriage (Miller 1998). Dr. Margo Prade, who worked as a family physician in Akron, had two beautiful daughters, Sahara and Kenya, with Captain Prade (WKYC-TV 2010). Following their divorce, according to Dr. Prade's babysitter, Captain Prade would question her extensively regarding Dr. Prade's whereabouts when she was not home (Miller 1998). In addition, coworkers of Dr. Prade stated that Captain Prade would repeatedly stalk her by sitting in his vehicle outside of her office building, and even went to the extent of making verbal threats to kill her (Miller 1998). I frequently saw Dr. Prade and her two children shopping at a local mall, where I worked an extra security job. Dr. Prade always made a point to go out of her way to come over to me and say hello while greeting me with a radiant smile. I always looked forward to seeing her, and was shocked when I learned of her heartless murder just a day before Thanksgiving in 1997.

Margo's lifeless body was found slumped behind the wheel of her minivan, which was parked behind her medical office building (Miller 1998). Margo was mercilessly shot five or six times with a .38 caliber revolver (WKYC-TV 2010). Bite marks were found on Margo's left arm; however, at the time of the murder DNA tests were not sophisticated enough to distinguish the killer's DNA from the enormous amount of blood Margo lost which saturated the bite impressions (Meyer 2010). Investigators thought they received a break in the case when they learned a neighboring business had a video camera pointing toward the homicide scene. However, after extensively viewing and enhancing the video footage, the suspect could only be seen as a dark shadowy figure approaching Margo's vehicle. Following Margo's death, Captain Prade maintained his innocence and stated that he was working out at the time of Margo's death as his alibi.

Shortly after the cold-blooded murder, Captain Prade agreed to take a polygraph test. Bill Evans, who conducted the polygraph, stated that Captain Prade registered deceptive responses on the questions "Do you know who killed Margo?" and a vital question concerning if he knew the specific caliber of the weapon used to kill Margo (WKYC-TV 2010). At the time of the polygraph, only Mr. Evans, former Chief of Police Craig Gilbride, and the killer knew that Margo was slain with a .38 caliber revolver (WKYC-TV 2010). Overall, Mr. Evans stated that Captain Prade did not do well on the polygraph test (WKYC-TV 2010). However, because polygraph results cannot be used in court, Captain Prade was not arrested and the investigation continued.

From the investigation, it was determined that Captain Parade took his stalking of Margo a step further by secretly recording her home telephone conversations without her knowledge (Miller 1998). In addition, two overwhelming pieces of evidence eventually led to Captain Prade's arrest and conviction. First, the bite mark impressions left by the killer on Margo's left arm was a direct match when compared to Captain Prade's lower teeth (Miller 1998). Secondly, investigators found a note Captain Prade wrote to himself six weeks before Margo's untimely death, which listed in detail his debts and how he would spend much of Margo's $75,000 life insurance policy he would inherit (Miller 1998). Additionally, Captain Prade would also benefit by gaining control of nearly $500,000, which his daughters would be entitled to in an additional life insurance policy (Miller 1998).

After much deliberation, the jury unanimously ruled that the evidence presented by the state proved beyond a shadow of a doubt that Douglas Prade viciously murdered his ex-wife Margo (Miller 1998). Captain Prade, who continued to claim his innocence throughout the trial, was sentenced to life in prison (Miller 1998). Judge Mary Spicer added an additional six years to the sentence for using a firearm in the murder and for recording Margo's home telephone conversations without her consent (Miller 1998). Following the guilty verdict, Captain Prade addressed the court by stating, "I did not do this. I am an innocent, convicted person. This has been an egregious miscarriage of justice. You do not have the luxury of relaxing. I absolutely did not kill Margo" (Miller 1998). When Captain Prade was found guilty, Margo's killing was vindicated; however, at the same time Margo's children were instantaneously left without either of their maternal parents to nurture them and placed in a whirlwind of feelings of anger and sorrow.

Another senseless tragedy occurred when Canton Police Officer Bobby Cutts Jr. viciously took the life of Jessie Davis and their unborn child, Chloe (Hoover 2009). Officer Cutts Jr. was married at the time of the savage murder; however, he was having extramarital affairs with several different women including Jessie, who he had a two-year-old child with named Blake (Hoover 2009). On June 14, 2007, Jessie Davis, who was due to give birth July 3, failed to show up for work (Juror Thirteen 2010). On June 15, Jessie's sister, Aubrey, and an associate sensed something was wrong and went to Jessie's residence to investigate (Juror Thirteen 2010). After arriving at the residence, they found two-year-old Blake alone inside (Juror Thirteen 2010). In addition, they were startled when they entered Jessie's bedroom and found it in disarray with her comforter missing (Juror Thirteen 2010). In fear for her sister's safety, Aubrey called 911 to report her sister's disappearance, and then telephoned Officer Cutts Jr. to inform him of the situation (Juror Thirteen 2010). Strangely, Officer Cutts Jr. showed up at Jessie's residence in full uniform at approximately 8:30 a.m. and informed Aubrey that he just got off his midnight shift (Juror Thirteen 2010).

Summit County Sheriffs immediately started an investigation and spoke with Jessie and Officer Cutts Jr.'s two-year-old son Blake, who told detectives, "Mommy was crying. Mommy broke the table. Mommy's in rug." (Juror Thirteen 2010). While Jessie's family posted over 1,200 fliers throughout the community—begging for anyone with information regarding Jessie's disappearance to come forward—the FBI and State Highway Patrol joined the investigation (Juror Thirteen 2010). The next day an all-volunteer organization out of Texas called EquuSearch joined the search with a mounted search and rescue team (Juror Thirteen 2010). After a week with still no leads, 1,500 citizens came together and organized a search around Jessie's residence, but their efforts did not result in locating Jessie (Juror Thirteen 2010).

After denying any involvement in Jessie's disappearance for a week, Officer Cutts Jr. led detectives to Jessie's lifeless body inside a Summit County Park (Hoover 2010). Canton Police Union Attorney, Avery Friedman on behalf of Cutts

Jr. stated, "He went to the scene. He saw Jessie Davis. She reached for his trousers. Her eyes rolled back and she died. He panicked. He called a friend. The friend came over and assisted him in the removal of the body" (Juror Thirteen 2010). Investigators knew the friend Attorney Friedman was referring to was Myisha Ferrell, who was a high school friend of Cutts Jr. (Juror Thirteen 2010). According to Ferrell's neighbor, investigators searched Ferrell's house and seized several bottles of bleach, three empty containers of fabric softener, a partial roll of duct tape, cell phones, and garbage bags (Juror Thirteen 2010). In gathering additional evidence against Cutts Jr., investigators reinterviewed Blake, who when asked about the incident, stated, "Daddy's mad" (CBS 2008). Unfortunately, the Summit County Medical Examiner was unable to ascertain the cause of Jessie's death or gather any possible DNA from the suspect off of her body, because Jessie's decomposed corpse was exposed to the scorching summer heat for nine days (CBS 2008).

Despite the medical examiner's lack of success and no concrete motive behind the killing, investigators had enough evidence to charge Officer Bobby Cutts Jr. with two counts of murder and place him on trial (Hoover 2010). During the trial, Myisha testified that she was tricked by Cutts Jr. who stated that he was going to pick her up because he needed a babysitter for Blake. However, when Cutts Jr. arrived at her residence, Cutts Jr. had Jessie's deceased body in the rear of his truck (CBS 2008). The prosecutor informed the jury that Cutts Jr. used bleach to cover up the crime scene and sprayed his truck down in a deceitful attempt to get rid of any evidence which would link him to the crime (CBS 2008). Cutts Jr. gave the jurors an unconvincing story that he sprayed down his truck because he wanted to get numerous bugs off of his windshield (CBS 2008). Cutts Jr. also contended that Jessie died when he accidently struck her in the neck with his elbow when she attempted to prevent him from leaving her residence (Hoover 2010). After Jessie's death, Cutts Jr. stated that he panicked when he decided to get rid of the body (Hoover 2010).

Based on Myisha's testimony, overwhelming evidence, and Officer Bobby Cutts Jr.'s multiple inconsistent statements, the jury found Cutts Jr. guilty for the death of both Jessie Davis and who was believed to be their unborn child, Chloe (Hoover 2010). Cutts Jr. was sentenced to life in prison with no chance of parole until he serves fifty-seven years (Hoover 2010). As a result of Cutts Jr.'s terrible actions, I could sense the loss of public confidence in the police even in my community. On several occasions following the arrest of Cutts Jr., citizens would adamantly express their concern to me that they felt afraid of police officers and certainly would not allow themselves to be alone with an officer under any circumstances. However, despite losing a lot of public confidence, a greater tragedy occurred when Blake was forced to watch his pregnant mother's death in the hands of his own father. As a result, Blake must now endure the psychological trauma placed on him by his father's heinous actions, and is left to fend for himself without the loving guidance of his mother, or the companionship of his soon-to-be sister, Chloe.

We have examined the devastation, which occurs at the family and community level when police officers commit the unthinkable act of murdering their loved ones. In comparison, when an officer is slain in the line of duty, their family suffers a catastrophe, which will impact them mentally for the remainder of their life span. Additionally, citizens within the community mourn the loss of a valued protector of their property and lives. I can recall one tragic incident involving a well-liked K-9 officer from a nearby city.

On July 13, 2008, at approximately 2:00 am, K-9 Officer Josh Miktarian informed his dispatcher that he initiated a traffic stop and gave the suspect vehicle's license plate number (Nethers 2010). Moments later, the dispatcher reported that he could hear arguing and loud popping noises coming from Miktarian's radio (Nethers 2010). Officer Quinn responded to the distress call; however, after arriving on scene he observed that the suspect vehicle Miktarian stopped was gone (Nethers 2010). Josh's cruiser was parked with its overhead lights on and the K-9 dog, Bagio inside, but Officer Quinn could not locate Miktarian (Corrigan and Tinsley 2008). Officer Quinn was heard on the radio frantically stating, "Josh, forty-five, where are you at?" (Nethers 2010). Finally, Officer Quinn located Josh lying on the ground by a nearby driveway and radioed to dispatch that an officer was down (Nethers 2010). Dispatcher Christine Franko immediately responded by saying, "Officer down. Officer down. Officer down." (Nethers 2010). Officer Quinn cautiously approached Miktarian and noticed he had multiple gunshot wounds to his face (Nethers 2010). Unaware if the shooter was still in the immediate proximity, Officer Quinn dragged Miktarian across the street to an area providing greater cover, and requested an EMS unit (Nethers 2010).

Additional officers quickly responded to the scene and searched the immediate area in an attempt to locate the suspect (Nethers 2010). The officers were unable to find the shooter; however, they did discover a pair of Miktarian's handcuffs and a Taser lying on the ground next to where he was originally found (Nethers 2010). Officer Vanek, who was working for the Bedford Heights Police Department, drove his cruiser to a former address that the owner, Ashford Thompson, of the suspect vehicle resided (Nethers 2010). After arriving on scene, Officer Vanek observed a vehicle with the same license plate that Miktarian had earlier relayed to the dispatcher, parked in the driveway (Nethers 2010). Officer Vanek heard a loud quarrel inside the residence. Sensing someone may be in immediate danger, he opened the residence door and observed an African-American male standing with his hands raised over his head and arguing with an unknown female (Nethers 2010). Officer Vanek then noticed that the male had a pair of handcuffs dangling from his right wrist (Nethers 2010). The suspect turned away from the female and became aware of Officer Vanek and bolted for the kitchen (Nethers 2010). Officer Vanek chased after him and tackled the suspect just inside the kitchen doorway (Nethers 2010). The culprit desperately struggled to break free of Officer Vanek's grasp (Nethers 2010). The suspect, later positively identified as Ashford Thompson grabbed onto the nearby refrigerator handle and attempted to pull himself up toward the stove (Nethers 2010). The handle of the refrigerator gave way and ripped from its hinges just as Officer Vanek looked up and observed a handgun resting on top of the stove (Nethers 2010). Officer Vanek, who was extremely concerned for his safety, desperately clasped onto the suspect until a backup officer arrived and assisted him in placing the offender in handcuffs (Nethers 2010).

Unfortunately, Officer Josh Miktarian died of multiple gunshot wounds, including four shots to his head (Nethers 2010). It was rumored on my department, and later specified in court by the Summit County Prosecutor, that after

Miktarian initially fell to the ground, the suspect stood over him and discharged his weapon execution style. The suspect, Ashford Thompson, was no stranger to the criminal justice system; he had prior arrests for driving under the influence and possessing a firearm inside of a liquor establishment (Nethers 2010). Ashford Thompson showed no remorse during his trial, which the jury deliberated for less than six hours before finding him guilty of the savage murder, and later imposing the death penalty on Thompson (Corrigan and Tinsley 2008).

Officer Josh Miktarian left behind his wife Holly, who worked as an Oakwood police officer, his three-month-old daughter Thea, and his K-9 dog Bagio (Corrigan and Tinsley 2008). Citizens showed their sympathy and support for Miktarian by creating a makeshift memorial at Twinsburg's city hall, which they decorated with colorful flower bouquets, balloons, American flags, pictures of Miktarian, and handwritten condolences (Corrigan and Tinsley 2008). Police officers and myself showed our support by attending Miktarian's wake and funeral. My entire shift of over forty officers drove our police cruisers to Josh's wake to honor the fallen officer. Tears streamed down my face as I approached the casket and observed a family photograph of Josh Miktarian, his wife and daughter, resting on an easel just before Josh's inanimate body. I offered my sympathy to his wife who was standing next to Josh's once lively body. I was even more shaken when I observed pictures of Miktarian posted, which showed him playing in his friendly rock and roll band and several other loving family photos. In addition, Josh Miktarian's funeral was the ultimate display of both police and citizen uniting in a mass show of support. Hundreds of police officers with their marked cruisers from multiple states joined the long funeral procession, as hundreds of grieving citizens lined the street on the way to Josh Miktarian's final resting place. Bagpipes played beside well-dressed honor guard representatives from various departments, as mourning officers and citizens filled the cemetery. The overwhelming support from police and citizens was enormous; however, Josh's tragic death had implications to possibly cause post-traumatic stress disorder to his family and responding safety personnel who were on scene at Miktarian's harrowing death.

Responding officers and paramedics who witnessed Josh Miktarian's gruesome condition cannot erase it from their memory and are forced to deal with the image and make sense of the tragedy. Hopefully, the safety personnel were offered and continually seek psychological counseling in their times of need or confusion. Two examples can be seen about how the responding personnel vividly observed Miktarian's dire physical state by looking at the trial testimony of two individuals. First, Officer Klien, who was a responding officer on scene, testified that he observed numerous bullet holes to Miktarian's head and blood everywhere (Nethers 2010). In a desperate attempt to render assistance, Officer Klien took off Miktarian's shirt, bulletproof vest, and duty belt; however, his efforts were to no avail (Nethers 2010). Second, Lieutenant John Dunn, a paramedic with the Twinsburg Fire Department, responded to the scene and stated that he observed "A hole about the size of a quarter above (Officer Miktarian's) left eye." Lieutenant Dunn further added that the injury was "incompatible with life" (Nethers 2010). Additionally, Lieutenant Dunn was horrified when he was on scene and realized that the K-9 officer was Josh Miktarian, who he knew and his children played with his K-9 dog, Bagio at his fire station (Nethers 2010).

From the senseless barbaric execution style murder of Josh Miktarian, police and community relations grew closer as citizens went out of their way to show they cared. For example, our department has an annual K-9 benefit called "Hogs for Dogs" which is a picnic-type atmosphere with plenty of food, drinks, and guest prizes. Radio stations and citizens willingly support the benefit, which raises money to buy police dogs, equipment, and make worthy donations to fallen officers' families. When our K-9 unit put on a fundraiser for the Miktarian family, an enormous showing of public support gave much-needed comfort to Holly and Thea Miktarian. Through public compassion and involvement, tragedies such as these can provide another outlet for the grieving family members to turn to in their time of need, possibly resulting in another ear to listen or shoulder to cry on.

Chapter 6

Direct Family Concerns

Thus far we have explored outside factors such as police structure, personal police decisions, and police biases that indirectly affect the growth and development of the inner-city family. Now it is time to focus on the infrastructure of the inner-city family and examine its contributions leading to the collapse of the family structure. When investigating the nucleus of the family, I have experienced it to be a very sensitive subject when attempting to assist youths in dealing with obstacles created for him or her by their parent(s) or other family members. Family members at the root of the problem tend to condemn the police or its organization as the ones solely accountable for the youth's problem rather than accept their contribution to the chaos within the family. Through my experience in mediating thousands of domestic calls involving inner-city families, I have learned that disorganization in areas such as dual-parent involvement and priorities will likely lead the youth to become susceptible prey to the flawed side of law enforcement. I find it common practice among inner-city parents to solely focus on the latter, which leads to the youth being repeatedly placed on a crumbled family foundation and told by the judge, parent, or social service worker to succeed in life. However, if the family structure is distorted, the youth is unable to build on this family surface because the root of hindrance, being a parent(s) or family members, has either not accepted ownership of their role, or has not made strides to fix their shortcoming. Therefore, regardless of the number of times the youth is placed back into the same warped environment, the outcome of aggravation and frustration from lack of success to build a solid family structure will be the same.

Since the beginning of time there was man and woman. Adam and Eve shared an apple and their sin together, and the caveman hunted in order to bring nourishing food home to his wife and children. This form of family structure, which seemed to work, was set in motion since the beginning of time. However, in today's complex world the simple family makeup has been pushed to the wayside by changing family values, twisted morals, and unkempt promises. The words "till death do us part" seem to hold little substance although spoken in front of hundreds and vowed to the most high and mighty. Single-parent homes seem to be the norm now, and seek to unravel the wits of even the most dedicated unwed parent. In a CNN.com article on April 8, 2009, it reported that in 2007, 28% of white females gave birth out of wedlock in the U.S. compared to 72% African-Americans and 51% Latinos (Ravitz 2009). These statistics are a mere reflection of the dire state inner-city minority families are in, and how children suffer as a result. For instance, out of several hundred juvenile arrests I made throughout my career, I can only recall a handful of times when I brought the minority child home and released him or her to a two-parent household. There was an overwhelming amount of times that the disruptive child was turned over to an overstressed single mother who had little resources to aid her in raising her child. I found that the intentions of most single moms I encountered did have the best interest for their child and wanted to see them succeed in life; however, with little or no involvement by the father, the child's male role model was left up to chance.

Throughout my career, I have encountered a plethora of extremely angry young African-American males. Through my conversations with the majority of the young males fifteen to twenty years, it was obvious that the root of their perturbation was a strong feeling of being unloved by their father. The majority of youths would frequently confide in me that the only ones who they felt loved them were their mother and crew, which were their tight-knit friends from their neighborhood. During my conversations, numerous young males would brag that they would focus their attention on how many different "bitches" they could get pregnant. This mindset can help account for the remarkably high teen pregnancy rates each year. In addition, the greater number of females from single-family homes I encounter had exceptionally low self-esteem from not having a father's guidance and love. As a result, the females would seek out this missing affection from any number of males who would show them the slightest amount of attention. Many of the youths I spoke with were street-level drug dealers, juvenile delinquents, or high school students. The vast majority felt no obligation toward their children because they felt a sense of entitlement not to care since their father abandoned them. I frequently would inquire if they intended on contributing financial support to help support their offspring. Almost all of the youths would have no forethought of providing for their offspring and would go out of their way to point out that "hustling" was how they usually made their money. Hustling—which consists of participating in criminal activities such as selling drugs or stealing cars—and the government cannot account for this cash. Some chilling statistics from drugwarfacts.org show that at midyear 2007, over 1.5 million children in the United States had a father in prison (Sabol 2008). In addition, African-Americans accounted for 4,618 per 100,000, compared to 1,747 for Hispanic and 773 for white (Sabol 2008). These elevated numbers are alarming among the minority fathers because even if these prisoners wanted to be a part of their child's life, their part would be limited by their confines.

Through my extensive time working in the inner city, it has become evident to me that the highest priorities among most individuals I encountered were the tangibles of life. Fancy cars with booming stereo speakers, the newest cellular phones, and sparkling jewelry seem to be as desired as stocks, bonds, and bloated 401Ks are within the middle and upper classes. I vividly recall an incident where I was dispatched to investigate the welfare of children possibly being left alone at home and allegedly had no food to eat. After arriving on scene, I spotted a relatively new black Cadillac Escalade in the driveway. The vehicle had large polished chrome rims and the vehicle's paint gave off a lustrous freshly-waxed shine. The pricey vehicle was parked in the gravel drive of a shabby cape-style home. The exterior of paint was flaking off exposing the original tattered wood. As I approached the residence, I noticed the mailbox was lying on the front porch just ahead of the crumbling concrete steps, and the front door screen was partially ripped away from the storm door and waved at me as the wind blew across its surface. After knocking at the door, a heavy-set African-American female in her midtwenties answered the door. She had long hair that was braided and at the ends were multicolored plastic beads, which rested on a designer shirt that overhung onto her stylish hip-hop patched jeans. Before I could explain the reason for my visit the female stated, "No one called, no punk ass police" and shut the door. I immediately banged my fist heavily against the door causing the house windows overlooking the front porch to rattle. The female opened the door and shouted, "Why are you harassing me?" In an attempt to calm her down, I lowered my voice and explained my reason for being there in a tranquil tone. The obese female rolled her eyes and loudly smacked her lips together before stating that she was presently home so everything was fine. I pleaded with her to allow me to enter the residence in order to check on her children's living conditions, and that my inconvenience to her would only be temporary. In my attempt to persuade her, I also informed her that if she were unwilling to cooperate, I would have to question her neighbors to see if they were knowledgeable about her living conditions. The stocky female slowly moved out of the doorway and with a sigh stated, "Come on in, and let's get this over with."

Once inside the residence, I can recall that the only furniture present on the entire first floor was a nicked-up kitchen table surrounded by three out-of-place vinyl chairs. The sunlight raced through the cracks of newspaper taped to the windows, which revealed a faint layer of dust, coating the naked table. I made my way upstairs and first viewed a bedroom with only a worn-out mattress on the center of the floor, and an abundance of name brand adult-sized clothing scattered about. The next bedroom revealed an infant child, approximately two years old, lying on a tattered bed comforter in the corner of the unfurnished room.

"He is fine. Leave him be," the husky lady exclaimed as I made my way around several strewed soiled diapers on the floor toward the child. The obese lady swiftly followed me in the room and began to slightly tug at the back of my uniform shirt in an attempt to prevent me from examining the toddler. I hurriedly hunched down next to the infant, while breaking free of her plump hand's grasp. Upon close inspection of the child, I was startled and instantly stumbled backward when I opened up the light blue comforter in which the child was nestled inside. Scores of cockroaches scurried out in various directions throughout the dimly-lit room. After hurriedly regaining my composure, I turned backward and flipped on the outlet switch, activating a single naked light bulb that hung from the ceiling. The commotion jolted the infant who let out a thunderous cry. I quickly swooped up the toddler and darted past the plus-sized female, leaving the cockroach-infested bedspread behind.

"Give me back my baby!" the female screamed as I disappeared into the last unchecked bedroom. The nude baby began to become placid as I held him gently against my chest. The last room displayed another bare mattress on the floor, surrounded by four walls, which had been heavily decorated by an unknown child's scribbling in crayon.

"Whose room is this?" I inquired to the overweight female who followed me inside.

"This is my daughter's room that is six years old and she is in school right now," she exclaimed.

"Now give me back my child," she demanded.

At this point, I gave the dispatcher a code that would cause her to start a backup unit to me. I did not want the obese female to struggle with me over the defenseless child, nor did I want the obviously upset female to attempt to pummel me first in order to get her infant son back. I explained to her that I needed to examine her kitchen before any decisions could be made regarding her child. She hesitantly complied and I went downstairs to inspect the kitchen for food. After opening the refrigerator with one hand and holding the infant with the other, I was briefly taken back to my childhood by the presence of free government cheese inside. Unfortunately for the children, this was the only item besides a plastic gallon of water inside. I inquired if she had any food present in the cabinets as my backup officer arrived on scene.

"I have plenty of food right here," she exclaimed as she opened up a cabinet revealing six packets of noodles.

I asked the heavy-set female to sit down and stealthily placed the backup officer between her and myself. I then attempted to explain to her that the infant and her child at school would have to be place in children services custody due to the deplorable living conditions. The stout female sprung up at once, causing her chair to tip backward and crash to the floor.

"The hell you are. You ain't taking my children nowhere!" she bellowed.

I replied, "Now calm down, this will probably only be temporarily. Just until you get back on your feet," I tried to convince her as she attempted to push past my backup officer to get to her child. The obese female refused to listen to numerous pleas I gave her to keep her composure; therefore, my partner had to place her in handcuffs until her aggressive behavior subsided.

Throughout my career, this experience mirrored a lot of my calls within the inner city in two areas. First, I found that a lot of individuals determined their wealth by what car they drove. I typically would see an exorbitantly priced car with polished rims in the driveway of a dilapidated house. On numerous occasions, upon entering the residence I would find little to no furniture; however, individuals would frequently call to report thousands of dollars in car stereo equipment stolen from their vehicle. Secondly, designer clothing for females and stylish jeans for the males were some of the most sought-after products in the community. These material items repeatedly hold down inner-city families who are struggling to make ends meet. Once they give into the peer pressures of the inner-city subculture to buy the pricey cars and clothing, they are locked into a debt, which takes away from the real essentials like food for their children or unexpected home repairs. The most cataclysmic part of this scenario is that it will continuously repeat itself unless the individual changes his or her priorities. The cycle consumes their money each time, as their purchased car will always depreciate in value, and their fashionable clothing wears or goes out of style. When many young African-American males stopped buying designer shirts and started buying plain colored T-shirts, I was enthused that they were no longer wasting much needed money on overpriced clothing; however, my elation was short-lived as the different colored shirts were soon used to identify with a particular gang on either side of the city. Some juveniles were slain based solely on being in the other side of the city while wearing the colored T-shirt of a rival gang. These senseless deaths leave the loved ones in a state of trauma, which they may never psychologically recover from.

Another event, which I frequently observed in the cycle, occurred when the individual's money was extended outward too much into the person's car and clothing; however, they still wanted furniture. This made them susceptible targets of the rent-to-own stores. The overrun individuals would quickly learn that if they failed to make a payment, their furniture would be repossessed without delay. I can recall talking to an owner of a rent-to-own store for furniture. He snickered when he told me that after the person puts up a down payment and pays the next three months, he hopes the renter doesn't pay so he can reclaim the merchandise and receive another down payment when rented again. Therefore, he further explained that the furniture is paid off at his wholesale price after the first three-month rental. I would attempt to educate the inner-city citizens of financial deception such as this, and preach to them to save for their furniture or electronics to avoid the high interests and steep down payments by the rent-to-own businesses. I can recall one of my best friends would sleep on a cot in college because he did not have the funds to buy a mattress and refused to solicit a rent-to-own establishment. Throughout my career, I would often express my disgust that these particular corporations, which would operate solely in the depressed areas and oppress the poor even further by locking them into high-interest debt. I could only attribute individuals within the community who patronized them as falling into the trap of Americans' present-day desire of immediate gratification or lack of education.

The youth needs to be taught how to plan and look forward to the future. I strongly feel that the inner-city youths need positive role models in their life to achieve this goal. The older role models, whether it is an aunt, uncle, grandparent, or someone from the Big Brother & Big Sisters program, can help get our children's future focused by showing them how far they came in life. The youth of today is inordinately stuck in the now, and does not envision the possibilities of what could lie ahead. It saddens me that through my numerous interactions with our inner-city youth, many feel it is exceedingly normal to either witness or become a statistic of a violent death.

In today's fast-paced world, it is extremely common to see both parents working or a single parent having to work two jobs in order to provide the mere essentials for their loved ones. If you throw in the usage of drugs, which some parents turn to in order to cope with their stress, it blends in a recipe for disaster within the home. Today in the United States, our children are decidedly frustrated and crying out to be heard through heinous acts of violence. These once unthinkable acts committed by children have uninvitingly touched virtually every American city. For example, in March of 2005, fifteen-year-old Deliesh Allen-Roberts patiently waited outside of Locke High School for her aunt to pick her up from an honest day of learning. Just before her aunt's arrival, known gang member Dejuan Harris, who was eighteen years old, opened fire with a gun at a rival gang affiliate. Tragically one of the bullets intended for the gang member struck and killed Deliesh (Palmer 2006). This senseless act also victimized Deliesh's family, friends, classmates, and community who were left behind to psychologically pick up the pieces in the aftermath of the numerous stages of grief.

Today, as gang populations swell in the inner city, more and more innocent bystanders are falling victim to gang members' villainous acts of violence. I found through my experience that the police could only solve a slight portion of violent crimes on their own. The complete cycle of the act, investigation, arrest, and prosecution rarely can be completed without community involvement. This proves to be a gigantic problem when open lines of communication between the police and public are broken from past indifferences. The police need the citizens to be their extended sense of sight and report and crimes they see, and additionally be willing to testify against the violator. On the other hand, the public needs the police to protect them from possible intimidation, brought on by the arrested party's friends or family members. It is only when both entities work together through trust and respect, that criminals will be successfully prosecuted and the neighborhoods given back to the children.

Our children's acts of bloodshed cannot only be seen in major U.S. cities, but also in the heart of America. In April of 1999, the well-known incident at Columbine High School forever changed parents' perception that their child was sheltered from any odiousness acts while at school. Seniors Eric Harris and Dylan Klebolds' detestable deeds of killing twelve students and one teacher at their Jefferson County, Colorado School was a premeditated plan that needed parent, police, and community involvement way before the incidents actually occurred (Toppo 2009). Getting involved in youths' lives every day through activities such as sports, after-school programs, community involvement, and open parental communication are just a few preventive ways to help stop the irrational future catastrophes that struck Columbine. Although there is no guarantee a particular intervention will work, we as a community must strengthen our efforts to guide and nurture our youth as a whole.

"It takes a village to raise a child," is a well-known African proverb, which urgently applies to today's western culture. To illustrate, the FBI uniform crime reports that in 2002, 2.3 million juveniles were arrested, accounting for 17 percent of all arrests. In addition, teenagers under eighteen years of age arrested for murder drastically jumped 150 percent from 1985-1994 (Snyder 2001). These figures support my plea for more public involvement. Throughout my career, I have personally seen juvenile violent crime impact my community. Just recently in my city, an incident occurred where an unsuspicious sixteen-year-old child was enjoying a summer day sitting on the front porch of his adoptive mother's residence. An unknown seventeen- to twenty-one-year-old African-American male approached the adolescent, according to a friend who witnessed the incident. The unidentified male pulled a handgun out of his waistband as he approached the unworldly sixteen-year-old and fired one shot into his chest while stating, "This is my hood." The suspect fled on foot from the scene, while the juvenile's friend yelled for his adoptive mother. After running out of the house to aid, the adoptive parent started CPR on her lifeless son. The adoptive mom vigorously attempted to revive her son as she performed compressions on his blood-soaked shirt. Unfortunately, the young boy passed away from the gunshot wound, despite his adoptive mother's acts of valor and love. The broad description of the suspect given by the victim's close friend was broadcast over the police radio and officers flooded the area looking to apprehend the killer. The meticulous search did not unveil the suspect's whereabouts; however, a police informant gave a suspect's name to homicide detectives a few days later. The detectives swiftly put together a photo array and rushed it out to the witness for a possible positive identification.

After arriving at the witness' residence, the detectives were stifled with an enormous roadblock when they learned that the juvenile had not been seen since the incident. Further questioning led detectives to suspect that the boy's parents had hidden him at another location, in order to both prevent the youth from possibly testifying against the killer and to protect him from the danger of becoming a second victim. I would be lying if I said I did not understand the parents' concerns for the child's safety. However, to both rectify the sixteen-year-old's death and to keep members of the society safe, the witness should be urged by the community to step forward. Therefore, the witness could receive protection and support from both the public and the police. As a result, the police are ultimately powered by the community, which it serves, and the community must trust those in which they empower. Without a true balance, the police and community will be at odds, and the criminals will thrive on this dysfunctional equilibrium of power.

Chapter 7

America: The Melting Pot

Inner-city neighborhoods have historically been flooded with new immigrants and struggling minority families, which harbor together in their attempt to live the American dream. The new families are instantly faced with financial stresses imposed just to provide for their basic essentials, and the emotional strain of leaving extended family members behind in their homeland. These newbie families have limited resources to aid them in their quest to establish their roots within the community that they reside. On the other hand, minority families who resided in the inner city for multiple generations may feel threatened by the growing number of immigrants overrunning their neighborhood. For example, this can be seen in many inner cities in southern California, where cities such as Watts or Compton—which was once heavily populated with African-Americans—have now been overrun with Hispanics. To illustrate, in 1980 Compton, California, was roughly 80 percent African-American; however, today it is nearing 70 percent Latino/Hispanic (Murungi 2010). Throughout my career, I saw the number of Hispanic and Laotian families swell within the inner city that I patrolled. As a result, the established families' sense of comfort ability is jostled and tensions rise with the increase of new immigrants. This promotes division among the different nationalities and has the tendency to cause the formation of racially exclusive gangs who strategically mark and protect what they deem to be their territory. In current times, a barbaric gang from El Salvador known as Mara-Salvatruch 13 or MS-13, is infiltrating U.S. neighborhoods and bringing fear and devastation to everyone who resides close to their newly marked territory (IPaer 2009). The territorial boundaries limit the legitimate struggling family in expanding out to seek employment or leisure activities within other ethnic neighborhoods, as safety becomes an issue. In addition, individuals from different cultures frequently practice customs and traditions from their homeland, which may clash with the pressures placed on them to adapt to Western civilization. Therefore, newly established families absorb an immense amount of pressure to conform, which can lead to bloodshed as the two cultures converge.

During my career, I can recall a repugnant incident involving a feeble Pacific Island mother, who was married with a six-year-old and a four-year-old daughter, and had established new roots in hopes of living a tranquil life in

Akron. The timid mother was drastically unhappy in her marriage and took her children to her husband's work—who was also an islander—and informed him that she intended on ending their marriage. The husband, who was working alone in a factory that incinerated steel at a sweltering 1,800 degrees, became infuriated with his wife's desire to sever ties. The husband struck his wife over the head with a blunt object, causing his wife to unconsciously pummel to the ground in front of their horrified children. The unsympathetic male dragged his wife's motionless body across the balmy concrete floor and laid her across the front loader of a forklift. With his children still watching in horrid disbelief, the husband slowly lifted her body up with the forklift and dropped his wife into a scalding 400-degree drum of oil. The barbaric father then took his dismayed children into a nearby office and tied the once trusting children up with rope. He informed the petrified children to wait twenty minutes before they attempted to free themselves from the rope which bound them. The father went back into the room and committed suicide by jumping into the same scorching oil drum he dumped his wife's body into.

The traumatized children managed to untie themselves and waited a few minutes before leaving the office area. After being unable to locate their parents, they left the factory and summoned help when a citizen driving by stopped to inquire if they were all right. The puzzled citizen telephoned police, and officers along with EMS responded. The oldest child informed an officer on scene that "Daddy placed mommy on the bus." After observing the contents of the factory, officers believed that the child was insinuating that the yellow forklift was actually the child's description of the "bus." Unable to locate either of the children's parents, the officers telephoned the manager of the factory to respond to the scene. Once on scene, the manager, paramedics, and officers closely inspected the area again for the missing parents. On a hunch, the factory manager pressed a button on the oil drum machine causing the metal strainer to rise out of the sizzling 400-degree oil. As the strainer was hoisted up, the two charred bodily remains of the once vibrant husband and wife lay dripping of scalding oil from their lifeless bodies. An autopsy was performed later by the Summit County Medical Examiner; interestingly the oil was so searing that no oil was found inside the husband's lungs, which led the examiner to determine that the oil was so hot that it killed the husband before he could even take a breath. The children were placed in the custody of Summit County Children's Services for placement into preferably a relative's home.

In another example of a domestic violence case committed within a tightly-knit culture, we can examine the grotesque killing of Aasiya Zubair Hassan in Orchard Park, New York (Leniham 2009). In 2004, Aasiya and her husband, Muzzammil Hassan, started Bridges TV, which was the first ever English language television station directed toward Muslim demographics (Thompson 2009). The Muslim couple sought to erase stereotypes between cultures and bring races closer together as a union between North America and the Middle East following the 9/11 attacks (Thompson 2009). However, at home, Muzzammil was living an extremely different life from which he portrayed on television. The husband allegedly had violent tendencies and a temper, which caused Aasiya to file for both divorce and a protection order against Muzzammil in February of 2009 (Thompson 2009). According to an employee at the television station, once Muzzammil was witnessed swerving his vehicle toward his wife's car, which was occupied by her and their two children, causing Aasiya's vehicle to veer off of the road (Thompson 2009).

Only days after the divorce was filed, Muzzammil walked into the Orchard Park Police Station and informed authorities that his wife was dead (Leniham 2009). He led police officers back to his office where they were disturbed to find Aasiya's lifeless body lying in an office hallway next to her decapitated head (Thompson 2009). Detectives determined that Aasiya was decapitated with hunting knives, and Muzzammil was charged with second degree murder (WIVB-TV). President Marcia Pappas from the National Organization for Women spoke out against the grisly murder and stated that Muzzammil's act was a terroristic version of a "honor killing" (Thompson 2009). Nadia Shahram, a teacher of family law and Islam at University at Buffalo Law School, gave valuable insight that honor killing is still widely accepted and practiced among radical Muslim men who feel betrayed by their spouse (Thompson 2009). Despite witness accounts of violent streaks and abuse toward his wife, Muzzammil claims that he was the one in the relationship who was actually abused. Muzzammil is currently awaiting trial and is adamant of his flimsy accusations of enduring physical abuse from Aasiya during their marriage (Leniham 2009).

The notorious serial killer Jeffery Dahmer can be examined regarding his targeting of minorities and how it intertwined with the need for officers to be sufficiently trained in foreign languages and professional mannerisms in relation to their contact with the public. Jeffrey Dahmer grew up in Bath Township, Ohio, where he savagely murdered his first victim, a hitchhiker, by bludgeoning him to death with a barbell just a few short miles from the city where I worked (Terry 1994). Later, Dahmer moved to Milwaukee where he predominantly handpicked African-American and Asian men and boys to lure back to his apartment with promises of giving them beer and cash in exchange for allowing Dahmer to take nude photographs of them (Terry 1994). In May of 1991, Dahmer convinced a fourteen-year-old Laotian boy named Konerak Sinthasomphone to accompany him back to his apartment (Terry 1994). While inside the apartment, Dahmer drugged and sodomized the child (Terry 1994). When Dahmer left to buy a six-pack of beer, Konerak ran into the street naked and bleeding from his rectum (Terry 1994). A neighbor named Glenda Cleveland telephoned police and expressed her concern for Konerak's well being, after her daughter and niece spotted the tormented boy (Cronin and Prud 1991).

After arriving on scene, the officers were unable to communicate with Konerak because he was allegedly high on drugs and that he did not speak English (Cronin and Prud 1991). Unfortunately, the responding officers were met by Dahmer who was returning home from the store, and when questioned by officers regarding Konerak's condition, Dahmer deceived authorities and told them that Konerak was his nineteen-year-old boyfriend and they were just involved in a lovers' quarrel (Terry 1994). The officers took Dahmer for this word and did not thoroughly investigate Glenda's uneasiness about the circumstances. Tragically, the officers did not speak Konerak's native language, nor did they ask for an officer who could translate on the police radio to respond to the scene to assist them (Terry 1994). Instead, they carelessly released Konerak into Dahmer's custody (Terry 1994). Glenda adamantly expressed her worries to the dispatcher for Konerak's safety by repeatedly calling back into police headquarters to inquire about the status and also informing a dispatcher that she believed Konerak was just a "child." (Cronin and Prud 1991). The dispatcher and the officers on scene did not take Glenda's concerns seriously. As a result, shortly after officers cleared the scene, Dahmer brutally killed Konerak

(Terry 1994). As many of you are aware, Dahmer continued to savagely murder, dismember, and have sex with the corpses of his victims, and frequently ate their flesh, until another potential casualty escaped from Dahmer and summoned police (Terry 1994). After seventeen grisly murders, Dahmer was arrested and his apartment was searched, where authorities found a 55-gallon vat used to decompose bodies, skeletal remains, and a refrigerator containing human hearts (Terry 1994).

The community's bond of trust between the citizens and officers was tragically severed from Glenda's pleas to aid Konerak going unanswered, and from the officers' lack to carefully investigate the matter before irresponsibly handing the child over to Dahmer to be slain. To add insult to the unforgiving situation, the officers who responded to the scene cleared the call on the police radio by making insensitive remarks such as stating that one of the officers was going to take his partner to the station "to get deloused" while laughter was heard in the background (Cronin and Prud 1991). From this sorrowing ordeal, police departments can see the valuable need for both foreign language and cultural sensitivity training for their officers. These practiced skills will aid them insurmountably in communicating effectively with minorities within the neighborhoods they protect.

The MS-13 gang maintains a stronghold on its territory throughout many large areas within both Mexico and American cities (IPaer 2009). Federal authorities believe MS-13 members operate in states such as New York, Oregon, Florida, Georgia, Texas, Nevada, Michigan, Alaska, Washington DC, and Virginia (IPaer 2009). The immense violence that MS-13 members use to establish themselves within a community can ruin any sense of safety or hope for the future that law-abiding contributing members of the communities had worked exceptionally hard to build (IPaer 2009). For example in 2003, MS-13 members were feeling pressure that the Honduras government was attempting to dissolve their gang through stringent organized crime laws (IPaer 2009). As a result, two MS-13 members armed with AK-47s and a MS-16 used their vehicle to cut off a public bus in traffic on a crowded Honduras street (IPaer 2009). The MS-13 members quickly entered the bus with their automatic assault rifles and opened fire on the innocent citizens, killing twenty-eight people including seven small children (IPaer 2009). The MS-13 gang members left their trademark calling card behind by placing a slang written note weighed down with rocks on the hood on the bus (IPaer 2009).

There will be several serious implications inner-city families will be faced with in the future as MS-13 gang members continue to grow throughout American cities (IPaer 2009). MS-13 members are known to engage in numerous criminal activities such as drug smuggling, murder for hire, selling stolen guns, arson, taxing store owners, and helping illegal immigrants get into the United States (IPaer 2009).

However, it is MS-13 members' savage acts of violence that will test our earlier discussed community programs such as neighborhood block watch programs, partnerships with community police officers, influences of role models, and active community programs. The community members and the police should be educated on MS-13 members' violent methods of operations, and develop additional programs or help from federal authorities to combat the gang members early on when they are first identified in their city (IPaer 2009). This preparedness can help neighborhood youth become aware and stay away from the MS-13's recruitment process, in which a potential member must either rape, seriously beat, or murder an innocent citizen in order to become a full-fledged member (IPaer 2009). Police officers should also be educated of the murderous potential MS-13 members have when they enter the United States and establish themselves in their cities. The MS-13 gang originated in El Salvador, with many of its members serving in the military as cutthroat guerillas during the civil war (IPaer 2009). Therefore, many MS-13 members have extensive training in fighting with machetes, which attributes to numerous beheadings of their adversary gang affiliates within today's Western society (IPaer 2009).

The frequently slayings of loved ones has touched virtually every class and culture in today's Western society. Families undergo dramatic stresses when jobs are lost to downsizing, expensive medical procedures are necessary, or unplanned children are born into already troubling relationships. With today's economy, jobs are scarce and home values are depreciating in practically every city in the United States. As families undergo these financial burdens, the strength of marital relationships is tested as divorce looms. With current technological advances, extramartial affairs are just a keystroke away with social sites such as Facebook or Myspace available for unhappy spouses to mingle. These stressors can lead to dejected feelings of being unable to provide for loved ones, overwhelming concerns of uncertainty regarding the future, and irate responsiveness of jealousy and disloyalty toward a spouse who is found to have given into temptation and ventured out of the once sacred vows of matrimony. With so many of these multiple impediments and financial encumbrances placed upon families, the character of every family member is tested as they weigh their options of reacting in a rational or drastically illogical way. Unfortunately, in many instances, without the proper intervention such as marital or financial counseling, a distressed family member may commit a dreadful act of taking their life and or the lives of loved ones. As a result, families are instantly torn apart and the survivors are left to work through the psychological anguish inflicted on them from the upheaval.

Chapter 8

Community Problems

Today, with so many broken homes, it is imperative that community programs, churches, and social service agencies get involved with inner-city families and become an extension of their family support system. These organizations must give families the tools they need to succeed in life through education, instilling values, providing role models, and serving as a mediator to families in domestic crisis. If offered, the struggling families must be willing to accept the much-needed help. Any past conflicts or community trust issues between the dysfunctional family and the conglomerates will lead to the family rebelling against any assistance no matter how extensive their need. On the other hand, when the burdened families and organizations work together in unison with the goal of strengthening the family, with each family that is built stronger, a more loving and safer community is established.

From kindergarten until eighth grade, with the exception of seventh grade, I religiously attended a Catholic school. Attending the required school mass on Fridays helped lay the spiritual foundation I have; however, by the eighth grade, I began to view the masses as systematically mundane. The structure was extremely predictable as the priest followed the same format consisting of sitting, standing, and kneeling during service at a set time. The priest's regimen was routinely composed of reading straight from the Bible in an uninspiring monotone voice. In addition, the elderly priest was seldom ever able to relate the Bible message to what the struggling families within the congregation were enduring. I searched other Catholic churches in an attempt to find a different style or priest who energized me to learn more about God; however, I found each church to have the same archaic structure with out of touch historic priests. I began to consider leaving the Catholic church, but was hesitant to venture out because I was reluctant to change. It wasn't until the mid-1990s when several priest sex scandals came to light involving young boys, that I undoubtedly became motivated to seek the fellowship of another denomination.

I was originally displeased because the priests and church structure, whom I observed, were not reaching out and inspiring troubled families in their organization. However, now I was livid at the numerous complaints being filed alleging that several priests were molesting young boys within their congregation. I felt betrayed that the priests, who originally did not motivate families, now were both physically and psychologically traumatizing them. In a recent example, the arrest and conviction of Priest Alejandro Flores in West Chicago shows how a priest's horrid misuse of a family's trust can lead to severe emotional anguish for the victim and his family (Stockinger 2010). The *Daily Herald* reported in September of 2010 that Flores pleaded guilty to one count of criminal sexual assault and was sentenced to four years in prison (Stockinger 2010). The Roman Catholic priest attempted suicide by jumping off of a church balcony after he learned he was under a police investigation for allegedly molesting a thirteen-year-old boy (Stockinger 2010). The most disturbing component of the entire episode is the fact that Priest Flores's supervisor witnessed the thirteen-year-old victim and his older brother change clothing in front of the priest and call him "daddy"; however, no disciplinary action was taken or additional restrictions placed on Priest Flores (Stockinger 2010). As a result, Priest Flores was free to continue his devious acts and later strip the innocence from the naive thirteen-year-old boy from St. Mary's church in West Chicago (Stockinger 2010). The trauma that Priest Flores caused extends beyond the victim, victim's family, and congregation, and reaches into the community causing an unnerving lack of trust for clergy. This feeling of skepticism can cause church members to withdraw from church, and deflect their feelings of atrocity and faithlessness they acquired from the incident, and place their irate sensitivities toward God. Therefore, from one priest's reprehensible actions, countless families are left with their spiritual beliefs in doubt, and they are subjected to an array of mixed feelings among family and church members, which can potentially disunite the parties involved. As a result, families lose fellowship among themselves and church members, thus hindering their chance to grow together as parishioners and as a community. Therefore, family members suffer because when tribulations arise they have less social support networks to help them cope and overcome any unrest.

After becoming flustered with the Catholic church, I set out to find a new and inviting church. I was instantly drawn into a gigantic mega church, deep in a poverty-stricken area of Warrensville Heights, Ohio. I had consistently heard the pastor on the radio preaching a solid message about helping out the community, and I was eager to attend and possibly get involved. My first day at the mega church was an eye-opener from the humdrum style of worship I was accustomed to in the Catholic church. The choir sung trendy gospel songs to several hundred worshipers who welcomed the song's inspirational lyrics by singing along or praising God out loud. When the pastor preached, I was roused with how he tied God's message into the obstacles most families are faced with today. By doing so, the pastor was able to direct church members how to solve their dilemmas through God's message. The pastor even gave out prepaid gas cards to church members to help mitigate the burden of everyday living expenses. I was delighted to see a pastor focusing the church resources on members of the community, and my first impression was that this was definitely the church for me.

For the next several months, I faithfully attended the mammoth church and observed my tithe money go to support less fortunate members of the community through items such as food, clothing, and shoe charity drives. To me personally, there was nothing more gratifying than seeing that the children within your community are being provided with the vital essentials of life. For once, I was elated to give my tithes and was looking into volunteering within the church, until a vicious rumor began to feverishly spread throughout the church. A few weeks earlier, I saw the pastor's daughter on the popular MTV channel, and she was celebrating her birthday on the show; however, church members were alleging that the party cost $500,000 at the expense of the worshipers. The pastor, who adamantly proclaimed that the birthday party only cost $25,000, and that it was paid for at his expense and not out of any church accounts, quickly quelled the rumor. Personally, I strongly believed the pastor was making such an astronomical amount of money through his mega church that he lost touch of the true value of a dollar. Regardless of which account the $25,000 came out of, the money could have gone a long way in doing God's work within the community. Numerous families' lives could have been touched and possibly changed by using the funds toward things such as counseling, after school youth programs, or job-training classes. For several weeks after the reckless spending, I attempted to place the incident out of my mind; however, I took it personal that numerous needy families were bypassed for an elaborate birthday party. As a result, I left the colossal church and attended an undersized neighborly nondenominational church closer to home.

My experience at the dainty church proved insulting to the struggling members of the congregation. During my second week at the church, I can recall sitting across from a petite African-American female who was dressed in a brown-stained long blue skirt with a gray-tinged blouse. I remembered that I was on a domestic dispute a month earlier involving the tiny female and her live-in boyfriend. The dispute quickly simmered upon police arrival; however, the females' living conditions is what I remembered most about the call. Wax candles burned to light the living room and kitchen of the residence where the electric had been shut off. In addition, two slightly filled buckets containing rainwater sat underneath two dripping holes in the kitchen ceiling. Numerous roaches cascaded across dirty pots and pans in the fiberglass sink.

While sitting across from the tiny female, the head deacon of the church stood up to address the members. He bluntly insisted that each member give an additional $100 with their tithes; for fifteen minutes he pleaded that the money would be used for the pastor and his wife's anniversary gift. I was instantaneously offended that he would put pressure on all of the members to donate, when I had firsthand knowledge that the dainty female sitting across from me was living a paltry life. In addition, I was out at the pastor's house a few months prior when he called to make a burglary report; I knew he resided in a lavish condo in an affluent neighborhood, and drove a new Mercedes Benz with expensive rims. Therefore, I was appalled that he would allow the church members to be literally coerced into spending thousands of dollars on an anniversary gift for him when members of his own congregation could not pay their own utilities, but were still faithfully placing tithes in the collection plate. I thought, how can this church help families outside of the church, when its pastor does not know what is going on with the families undergoing hardships within the congregation. When the deacon started the collection basket around, the destitute female hesitantly took the basket with a blank stare. Her hands slightly trembled as she peeked up to see if anyone noticed that she did not have the $100 gift the deacon asked for.

"Here, this is my gift to you," I stated to her as I handed her a crisp $100 bill.

The tiny female's eyes quickly filled up with tears as she whispered, "Thank you," with her mouth hanging open.

I then continued to walk out of the church doors and never returned to the avaricious church again.

My experiences with inner-city churches whether it be a mega or small church; a Catholic, Christian, or Non-domination belief, is that today's churches seem to be mostly run from a business perspective. Business savvy is truly needed in this day and age to stay afloat; however, when pastors or priests operate for profit is when the families within the community suffer. As a result, the faithful tithe money that was given to assist in doing God's mission in the community is instead used for needless luxurious items such as extravagant church entrances and private jets for some mega church pastors. This ill-spent money could be used for more useful activities such as inner-city medical mission work, job training classes, motivational speakers, safety and after school programs which would contribute to uplifting the community. In addition, pastors and priests must make a pronounced effort to get out into the communities where their members live and find out what struggles the families are currently enduring. If your church leaders are currently accomplishing these tasks, please continue your fellowship with that church and I urge you to stay involved with the families of your community through your congregation. However, if you have a friend or family member who belongs to a church that does not take these proactive steps to impact family's lives in a positive way, do not attempt to get them to come to your church, instead encourage them to transform their church thus touching numerous families lives and shaping their own community.

Throughout my career, I have encountered numerous members of the society who did not have an immediate family; however, they had an enormous wealth of knowledge and compassion to offer. I frequently urged them to volunteer to help a youth or family within their community. Programs such as Big Brothers and Big Sisters, with whom I volunteered, had a two-year wait list for role models of both boys and girls when I started at the organization. In addition, I advised citizens that area hospitals usually had a vast assortment of fulfilling jobs within the hospital, open to volunteers willing to get involved. Before I started nursing school a few years ago, I volunteered in the spiritual health center at one of our local hospitals. I was responsible for going to new patients' rooms throughout the hospital, and seeing if the patient needed a priest, chaplain, or wanted to confide in me or pray with me. I can recall working a homicide scene, getting off work, then seeing the victim's family while working my volunteer shift. As a result, my work hours were long, but my aching muscles were far outweighed by the opportunities I had to be a reflection of God and make a lasting impression on people's lives. I frequently shared my uplifting volunteer experiences with the citizens and urged them not to allow the interpersonal gifts God gave them to be wasted on idle time, but to use them to enliven their community.

Many inner cities such as mine have individuals whose hard work ethic and athletic ability enables them to become professional athletes. From my neighborhood alone, basketball phenom Lebron James and football greats Antonio Winfield and Beanie Wells grew up. These players excelled in their sports and were all rewarded with stardom and astronomical monetary contracts. Individuals like these who come from underprivileged areas must not forget their roots and leave their hometown communities behind. They have the monetary resources their old neighborhoods need to start large-scale programs such as a battered women's shelters, at risk youth group homes, and up-to-date job training programs. Unfortunately, other than Lebron James repaving neighborhood basketball courts and his annual Bikeathon—where hundreds of bicycles are given to indigent kids—I have not seen any visible charity work by the professional athletes from the city which I grew up and reside. I find it atrocious that I have observed some professional athletes return to the same impoverished area where they grew up and charge youths a fee to attend a sports camp, which they organized and instructed. Numerous children were left frustrated by their pauper circumstances when they were unable to attend because their parents could not spare the entry fee. As a result, the professional athlete indirectly causes turmoil between the child and his family thus offending the families who most need the help that the athlete is capable of providing. Through starting community programs or by being a role model, the professional athlete can play his or her part in revitalizing the community where they grew up and inspiring residents to get involved.

A large portion of the responsibility to raise a child is the obligation of the parents; however, it is not the only means available. Other avenues, such as vital community programs, active churches, and positive role models help shape the child's character and give him or her hope in life. Therefore, if the parent(s) could not adequately provide for their child in a physical or psychological area, then the individuals from the community who are involved in the child's life will be aware of the deficiency and provide the necessity. When working with volunteers, the majority of them feel immensely fulfilled when they aid a child, because the child is frequently placed in a hardship by someone else's actions, like a parent using drugs, which is out of the youth's control.

Chapter 9

Time for a Change

With the vast amount of stress placed on today's modern family, it is imperative that they are both educated on the factors contributing to the family's deterioration and given the necessities to combat the risks. Some help that strained families may receive comes from police programs, churches, and legislators. As a result, parents will be given the opportunity to gain valuable tools to help reconstruct the area of its breakdown. In addition, the parent(s) will be able to successfully adjust to future obstacles and keep their family functioning in today's complex society.

Police programs are vital in teaching families within the community about safety and improving public relations. This allows the police to gain citizens' understanding of a police officer's role in the public, and the resident's cooperation in helping deter and solve crimes. The fundamental plan of action that enables police and citizens to work together in their pursuit of making neighborhoods safer is through the block watch program. When ran efficiently, volunteers within a district can feel a strong sense of ownership to their own neighborhood as criminals get arrested and the crime rate falls. During my career, I have personally seen citizens watching out for criminal activity and relaying the valuable information such as suspect descriptions and suspicious vehicle's license plate numbers to the police, which reinvigorated several crime-ridden areas. Some neighborhood block watch leaders take it a step further and assign volunteers to a set shift to walk the neighborhood.

Early in my career, I remember patrolling an area of the city that was overrun by apartment buildings. The parking lots were crammed with vehicles because the majority of them did not have a garage. The exposed cars drew a lot of thieves to the area looking to break into the cars to steal any valuables. As a result, I was taking scores of reports for stolen stereos, laptops, and vehicle theft reports. I had spoken with many victims about starting a neighborhood watch program to deter these crimes and gave several citizens the phone number to our community-policing department, who would assist them in starting the program.

Unfortunately for one female jogger, the neighborhood watch was never started. The young avid jogger went for a run throughout the apartment complex as part of her morning ritual. During her jog, she was struck by a vehicle and pummeled to the unyielding pavement after being propelled off the front bumper and windshield of the vehicle. The driver of the motor vehicle exited his car and approached the female whose shallow breaths indicated she was still clinging to life. The remorseless driver grabbed the distressed female and dragged her into the nearby woods. Once inside the secluded area, he placed the jogger face down in a sizable rain puddle. The driver then fled the area and never reported the incident to police. Summit County Medical Examiner Marvin Platt ruled that the once vibrant jogger died from drowning as a result of her being placed face down in the water, and also suffered "blunt force injury to the chest and abdomen" (Cincinnati. com 2000). If the driver had not dragged her into the wooded area, or if a neighborhood watch program was put in place and a volunteer witnessed the incident, the active jogger would probably still be alive.

As a result of the senseless homicide, the crime scene was processed in hopes of gathering suspect or vehicle information. Crime scene detectives did a phenomenal job locating a trace amount of glass on the road where the victim traveled. As a result, it was determined that the victim caused the windshield of the suspected vehicle to crack when she thrashed into the glass. In addition, there was a minuscule piece of bumper left at the scene which was light green in color. The bumper was sent to the crime lab for analysis and it was determined that the vehicle which struck the jogger was a Mercury Topaz. The chief of police quickly went on the offensive and placed several officers on special details in the area with the sole purpose of locating the suspected vehicle, which would hopefully lead to the killer. Several weeks went by without any leads in the case. Detectives called numerous auto repair and glass shops in the area looking for a light green vehicle matching the known damages, but their efforts were to no avail. Amazingly, it was an officer who was patrolling the same apartment complex where the youthful jogger was murdered, who spotted a light green Mercury Topaz with a tiny piece missing from the front bumper. The fragment of bumper recovered from the homicide scene matched perfectly to the suspected vehicle.

The owner of the vehicle lived in the same apartment complex, and it was later determined that he was traveling to work, at the same time en route, on the morning which he struck and killed the vulnerable female. Through further investigation, detectives learned that the vehicle's owner drove the car to Pennsylvania to replace the windshield. The timing of locating the vehicle and his arrest was essential, because it was later learned that the perpetrator had an airplane ticket already purchased to move outside of the country only days following his arrest. Although the suspect was arrested and successfully prosecuted, I always wonder if the innocent jogger's death may have been prevented if an organized neighborhood watch program was in effect.

To illustrate the power motivated citizens have in solving crimes and aiding the police, we can examine the famous murder mystery involving killer Manuel Gehring. Gehring was undergoing domestic problems and had taken his fourteen-year-old daughter and eleven-year-old son out to enjoy the July 4 fireworks in Concord, New Hampshire (Kropko 2005). The children were never returned home to their mother's New Hampshire residence, and a week later Gehring was arrested in California without the children in his company (Kropko 2005). Through interrogation, Gehring stated, while en route to California, he pulled over on the side of the road, then shot and killed his children (Kropko 2005). He further stated that he drove for hours before pulling off of Interstate-80, and buried the children (Kropko 2005). Gehring gave valuable clues such as making two crosses out of sticks and duct tape and then placing a cross on each of the graves he dug for his children (Kropko 2005). Gehring also stated that there were bell-shaped sewer connectors, a fence, and woodpile in the area of the graves (Kropko 2005). Manuel was unable to pinpoint the exact location of the graves and could be of no further assistance to investigators after committing suicide by hanging himself inside of his jail cell (Kropko 2005). In 2004, the US Geological Survey conducted an analysis on the soil found underneath Gehring's vehicle and soil near a shovel inside his car (Kropko 2005). It concluded that the soil most likely came from Northeast Ohio (Kropko 2005). With thousands of square miles in the region, the task of finding the childrens' bodies seemed insurmountable; however, the perseverance of a grocery store clerk proved to be the most valuable asset to the FBI and local authorities.

While working patrol, I received a call to meet a female reference a possible homicide site. After arriving on scene, I was greeted by a middle-age female who was standing in a vacant field with her Boxer-Rottweiler mix dog, just off of the highway. The female informed me of the Gehring murder and described the clues that he left investigators. The rambunctious female believed that based on the hints, she had found the area where the children were buried. We searched the area for the gravesite; however, despite seeing bell-shaped sewer connectors in the area, we were unable to locate the children's resting place. After not observing a woodpile, fence, or makeshift crosses marking the graves, we determined that it was not the burial location and the search was called off. I asked the female what motivated her to search so hard for the children. The driven lady told me that she worked long hours as a grocery store clerk to provide for her children, which she loved so much. She further stated that God placed it in her heart that the children's mother loved her missing kids just as much, and she wanted to bring them home to give their mother peace. Before I left the area, I wished her luck in finding the children but commented that her chances of finding the children, without a massive search team, was one in a million.

The persevering female continued her quest to locate the missing children and expanded her search to Hudson, Ohio, which is approximately ten miles outside of Akron. Three long months after I initially helped her look for the graves, the unwavering female and her dog found two shallow graves off an access road in Hudson (Kropko 2005). The area was consistent with all of the clues Gehring had given authorities before his death, and underneath the homemade twig crosses with duct tape lay the children's decomposing bodies (Kropko 2005). The Summit County Medical Examiner performed autopsies on the children and determined that Gehring's daughter was shot three times in the head, and her brother was shot once in each arm, his head and neck (Kropko 2005). The children's bodies were later returned to their sympathetic mother for a proper burial, which gave some closure to the horrendous act.

The determination of one female who set out with the single purpose of finding the children proved how willpower can lead to both accomplishing your goal and easing family's burdens. When you think about the strong-willed female's chances of finding the gravesite out of the thousands of uninhabited miles of rough terrain present in Northeast Ohio, it is nothing short of a miracle. The children's deaths were not totally in vain, because as a result of the incident, numerous citizens including myself had their faith in God grow to an insurmountable level. If one organized person could accomplish so much, imagine the progress an entire block watch team could make if they had a similar tenacity to tackle their neighborhood problems.

Gun safety classes are another way to both save lives and keep families intact. These classes enable police officers to teach their gun safety skills to citizens while at the same time establishing a working relationship with them, which can lead to a greater extent of the citizens' trust and involvement in police programs such as block watch programs. Beyond the benefit of citizens' willingness to get involved in combating crime in their neighborhood, priceless lives will be saved if the citizens utilize the safety techniques taught to them. For instance, unsecure guns within the reach of children prove to be a serious potential for disaster. Within numerous communities, you learn from news stations or the morning newspaper that an unsecure gun resulted in a child believing the gun was fake, pointing the loaded weapon at their friend or sibling, and pulling the trigger. The end result is a family which can never be the same physically or mentally again. To combat this frequent tragedy, the gun safety classes should not only teach the consequences of leaving weapons unsecure and within the reach of their loved ones, but gun safety locks should be given away to the citizens at the classes as an extra precaution and a way to reinforce the tragedy that can occur without taking the necessary prevention.

Another fatal mistake among citizens handling firearms entails placing their finger inside the trigger guard when moving their gun. This was a common mistake I observed throughout my career and believed it was done out of the thoughtless habit from playing childhood games such as cops and robbers. I can still vividly recall my friends and I, as adolescents, running around the backyard playing the game while never taking our pointer finger off the trigger of our plastic guns. Without firearm safety training, many individuals carry this unsafe habit with them as adults, only this time they are handling deadly guns. As a result, if the citizen trips or is startled while moving the firearm, he or she will instinctively flinch and pull the trigger resulting in a potential calamity.

I recall receiving a dispatched call to respond to assist EMS with a male who possibly shot himself on accident. After arriving on scene, I observed a rifle lying on the bedroom floor with several pieces of plaster scattered around the gun. The ceiling absorbed the majority of the impact as the round from the rifle caused approximately a six-inch in diameter hole in the plaster, exposing the wood joists underneath. The resident was a middle aged man, who was in a state of duress as he was panting, while sitting back in a recliner just inside his bedroom, creating a risk of hyperventilating. After quickly unloading and securing the rifle, I approached the resident and became nauseated to find that his flesh and part of the gentleman's skull from the top of his forehead had been blown off exposing a section of his brain.

"Remain calm, EMS is on their way," I informed him while I had to reinforce my trembling knees against the chair. I could see bone fragments from his skull clinging to his blood-soaked hair. I grabbed a nearby shirt, folded it up, and applied pressure with it to the citizen's gaping wound.

EMS arrived and immediately after seeing the extent of his injuries, they whisked the resident away to the hospital. Unaware if the incident was a botched robbery, attempted suicide, or accident; I photographed the scene and placed an officer there to guard the house, while I went to the hospital to continue the investigation. Before extensive surgery, the victim informed me that he was moving his rifle from the living room to the bedroom when he tripped over the corner of his mattress, which was on the floor, and accidently pulled the trigger of his weapon causing the self-inflicted injury. I spoke to his girlfriend and family members separately, who were waiting in the recovery room, and they all stated that the resident was not involved with any disputes or feeling depressed to their knowledge before the incident.

After gaining valuable information, I drove back to the residence and attempted to piece together what had transpired. I examined and photographed the mattress on the bedroom floor. I could see from the settled dust that the mattress was slightly moved, indicating it was possibly tripped over as the resident alleged. In addition, the angle at which the round struck the ceiling supported the middle-aged man's insistence that the discharge was an accident. Furthermore, I found an area in the living room corner that was free of dust which matched the dimension of the butt on his rifle, indicating that the gun was indeed originally in the living room as explained. Through a thorough investigation, it was determined that the incident was an accident; fortunately it was not a gruesome fatality. The resident's action of placing his index finger inside the trigger guard of even a long rifle, is one of many examples I have seen throughout my career involving this habitual error in judgment. The citizen was only attempting to move his rifle into the next room and almost resulted in his death. As a result, his family would have been left to wonder what actually transpired, while at the same time attempting to deal with and mourn their loss. From this example, it is clear that if the gun safety classes save just one life, they are indeed worth their cost.

Police departments should also establish a solid DARE program within its department. By becoming active in the inner city this program can prove beneficial in positively influencing youth through activities such as writing and art contests and building relationships by running recreational sports leagues. From this close involvement with our children, they will feel more at ease to reveal and confide their troubles with the officers participating in their neighborhood diversion programs. For instance, some of the youths' concerns may be unspeakable such as a family member touching them inappropriately. However, the DARE program's involvement in the neighborhood would create a level of trust and security for the child to disclose the deplorable crime to the officers.

When organized and equipped with dedicated officers, a DARE program can keep numerous children from becoming future victims by both keeping them involved in legitimate activities and giving them a resource officer to divulge their problems. Unfortunately, my department threw away these numerous opportunities to save children from being victimized, and giving them something positive to look forward to in their neighborhood, when the chief of police disbanded the unit out of spite. An officer of the DARE unit wrote a professional letter to the police union's newsletter, which was published, regarding his disapproval of a recent decision made by the police chief. As a result of the officer exercising his freedom of speech, the chief of police took the matter personal and sent several members of the DARE unit back into the patrol division to answer calls for service as his form of punishment. This action unfairly compromised children's safety and limited future cooperation from them as the close alliance between the DARE officers and neighborhood youths was callously demolished.

To further fortify the community through education, police departments should offer citizen police academies. These valuable schools can train individuals in an array of skills to properly identify crime and the necessary steps taken to prevent it. In a dire situation, if a citizen witnesses a crime occurring, the trained citizen will be able to remain calm and relay crucial information to the police dispatcher. These schools also build a tight-knit partnership between the community and police officers, and enhance the citizens' understanding of the stresses and dilemmas officers endure on a daily basis. For example, during my department's citizens' police academy, the individuals are given a fake laser gun and allowed the opportunity to interact with various staged scenarios on a large projector screen. The screenplay is realistic of a call which an officer would encounter and requires the citizen to determine if they would shoot in each scenario, and has them actually fire their replica gun when they deem necessary. After each scene, the computer shows the citizen where their shots would have hit if they discharged their weapon and the training officer critiques their action. It is amazing to see the citizen's reaction when they shoot an unarmed suspect or an innocent victim. The citizen is instantly made aware of the consequences of the everyday split-second decisions officers are faced with. As a result, the naive citizens usually gain a better appreciation and understanding of the stressful job officers perform.

Through community programs, officers can identify the citizens willing to get involved and put forth the tiresome effort to make their community a safer place to live. After distinguishing these individuals, neighborhood block watches can be formed and managed within the neighborhoods.

The block watch members will have obtained the necessary adeptness from the discussed police sponsored community programs, to recognize and thwart crime in their neighborhood. For example, block watch affiliates will be taught how one vacant house in their neighborhood could enable crime to skyrocket if they don't make a conscious effort to keep an eye on the empty habitation. The deserted residence allows criminals the opportunity to do covert acts such as selling drugs hidden from the police, engaging in prostitution, or using it as a refuge to bring an abducted victim. As a result, the block watch members must take on the measures of calling the police if they observe individuals entering the dwelling, checking the residence during daytime hours to ensure that doors and windows are securely boarded up, and working with the public health department in getting the desolate house torn down.

A terrorizing crime involving an uninhabited house occurred when I was a child, just a block away from the street I routinely played touch football. The reprehensible crime started in a neighboring city when the suspect, Samuel Herring, approached the victim, Phyllis Cottle, and forced her into her vehicle by threatening her with a knife (Cardwell 2009). Cottle attempted to summon help from nearby bystanders by screaming and blowing the horn of her vehicle as she was forced into the passenger seat (Cardwell 2009). The citizens who witnessed her cries for help dismissed her actions as a domestic quarrel and did not attempt to intervene or telephone the police (Cardwell 2009). Cottle was then forced to withdraw cash from a nearby bank, and was taken to a vacant house in my neighborhood and repeatedly raped (Cardwell 2009).

After being desecrated, Cottle was forced back inside her vehicle and taken to a nearby highway where Herring stabbed her in both of her eyes, lit the vehicle on fire, and locked Cottle inside to die. Herring fled the area on foot and miraculously, despite not being able to see and battling the heat from the immense flames, Cottle managed to unlock a door and fall on onto the ground (Cardwell 2009). The aftermath of the brutal attack left Cottle blind, and she was unable to identify her attacker (Cardwell 2009). I can still remember, shortly after the incident, the police driving around my neighborhood attempting to locate the vacant house where Cottle was sexually assaulted. Word quickly spread that when Cottle was being violated she looked out the window of the uninhabited house and observed a gray house with white trim and a decorative eagle emblem near the top. The police meticulously organized a search of the city to locate the house, but their efforts originally came up empty. Finally, a patrol officer, who several years later became chief of police, located the abandoned house. The house that Cottle saw with the decorative eagle was at an angle and was actually on the next block over, making its identification difficult for police. Soon after locating the house it was learned that the owner's son was Samuel Herring, who was eventually arrested and convicted of the grisly crime.

In relation to the described tragedy, you can see why there is an emphasis placed on block watch leaders to be aware of empty houses in their neighborhood and ensure that they remain securely locked or boarded up. Ideally, it is preferred for the block watch leaders to identify these homes and work with community police officers and city council members to enforce city ordinances requiring the owners to maintain their property. Although the process of holding landlords and property owners accountable is tedious, ensuring the safety of our children playing in the area is incomparable. Eventually if the block watch leaders, police, and city council work together in collaboration, the uninhabited houses not brought up to code will be torn down. The end result will be a sense of accomplishment for the block watch members, and a safer neighborhood for the families who reside there.

Another police-initiated activity that solves many crimes and reinforces a close partnership between the citizens and the police occur when officers follow up on their calls for service. Many police departments such as mine are stretched thin in manpower, resulting in an abundance of waiting calls. Despite being overburdened, the officers should make a conscious effort to follow up on the victim's criminal reports by interviewing possible witnesses and suspects. Merely taking a victim's report and immediately forgetting about it after the officer responds to the next waiting call is unacceptable. I frequently conveyed this to the patrol officers who worked my sector; as a result, the officers followed up on their calls, and if needed, they were placed on a special detail to accomplish their mission. Through their efforts, several crimes, which would have gone unsolved, resulted in an arrest; the victim was given a sense of closure, and the citizens within the officers' district were elated with the service provided. In addition, I found that as a supervisor, it was integral to follow up with citizens who called the police to determine if they were pleased with the service they received from my officers. Only a minute number of over one hundred sergeants on my department routinely performed this activity. By getting the citizens' opinion regarding the officer's job performance, I was able to give feedback to the officer enabling him or her to make corrections when necessary or to praise them if warranted, and the citizens felt reassured that they were an important part of the community.

One area, which I was guilty of neglecting my community, occurred when I traveled to Ecuador with members of my church for a medical mission trip. Although we helped over 1,400 residents with dental, visual, and medical needs, the cost of the trip cost nearly $3,000 per person. Reflecting back, I strongly feel that the money used would have gone a lot further by conducting a medical clinic in the impecunious areas of my own city. Therefore, church leaders and members should weigh the advantages and disadvantages of overseas versus local medical missions. With today's deplorable economy, the rising unemployment rate, and the surging poverty rate, a powerful argument can be made to aid America's cities. By supporting our own communities, children will gain much-needed medical and vision treatment, such as eyeglasses—which will allow them to accomplish more in school, read a bedtime story, or play sports with their friends.

Today's parents must take a more active role in their child's life and not depend primarily on the school system or the church to instill the necessary values and morals in their child. While working for the police department, I was on a report call for a stolen car stereo when the caller's daughter returned home from school and asked the caller, her mother, if she could help her with Algebra homework. The stumped mother just shrugged her broad shoulders and stated, "I never understood that stuff when I was growing up either." The puzzled mother offered no assistance to the daughter as the defeated daughter sluggishly made her way upstairs to her bedroom. From watching this interaction, I was infuriated that the mother did not offer support for her daughter's request; even if the mother was ignorant in the field of mathematics, she could have made an attempt to call a relative who was proficient or arranged a tutor through the child's school. The mother's lack of competency was no excuse for her lack of willingness to get involved in her child's studies. From her repulsive actions, the child is obviously placed at risk to continue the cycle to inadequately develop in school.

Parents should talk to their children about their past and not be ashamed to share with their unworldly offspring. Children love to hear heroic stories and parents love to be shining examples of success and triumph to them; however, children need to hear their parents' mistakes too and how they overcame the obstacles. As a result, children can learn from their parents' mishaps and gain a sophisticated sense of the world. Therefore, when youths become tempted by similar tribulations, they will be prepared with the knowledge to triumph. Additionally, the parent's involvement can help their child resist the appeal from many of today's rap songs and video games, which glorify grave mistakes such as robbery and murder.

Parental involvement should also extend to overseeing that their child is treated fairly if they have an encounter with the police. If both parties respect each other, the interaction will usually result with no antagonistic feelings toward one another. However, in instances when police officers abuse their power, the parents must take it upon themselves to initiate a formal complaint against the officer(s) involved. Formal complaints are investigated thoroughly by supervisors on my department, and if the grievance could not be proven due to lack of evidence—such as credible witnesses or video footage—the grievance remains in the officer's personnel file, which may deter a deviant officer from future incivilities or will serve as a red flag to supervision if the officer's complaint file grows. To illustrate, on my department, a mischievous police officer was repeatedly defending various questionable actions during citizen complaint investigations against him. One complaint, which was proven and led to his dismissal, involved the officer approaching a teenage girl, who was wearing a decorative beaded necklace at a family function, and going into explicit detail about what women at Mardi Gras must do to receive beads. A citizen grievance such as this proves extremely beneficial in identifying problem officers and enables the administration to discipline or terminate the officer, thus ensuring the safeguarding of its citizens.

In today's struggling economy, it is imperative to have a clean criminal background when applying for gainful employment. However, while working within the inner city, I found many of the youths had felony convictions for either drug possession or domestic violence on their record. These young men have limited options available to them because most employers refuse to hire individuals with felony convictions. Therefore, even if the individual completed a specialized job training program, the odds of them obtaining employment upon completion is minuscule. I personally encountered this barrier shortly after I was charged with my felony steroid possession charge. While on the police department as a sergeant, I was accustomed to earning over $32 an hour; however, following my arrest, I was turned down for employment at countless $7.30 an hour factory jobs and an $8 an hour telemarketing job. No wonder so many of our youth who obtain felony convictions turn to drug sales to provide for themselves and their family. Therefore, legislators and community leaders must be active in supporting diversion programs for first-time nonviolent offenders, so their record may be dismissed upon completing a court ordered program. In addition, upon completion of the diversion program, the offender must be taught how valuable this second chance opportunity is for their future employment chances. With the proper guidance and education, the youth's record will be erased, freeing them from a cycle of crime, and they will become law-abiding contributing members of society.

In conclusion, it is important to realize there are issues that police officers, police organizations, family members, and community leaders handle erroneously that negatively affect the growth and stability of today's inner-city families. A person must be thick-skinned to accept criticism and be able to look oneself in the mirror and evaluate him or herself to determine what area, which I discussed, does he or she fall short in. If the individual merely focuses on the issues raised which does not apply to him or her, then the person will not accept their responsibility to make the necessary changes to improve the areas which they are lacking that can be detrimental to the family's lives that they touch. Through identifying these shortcomings and making necessary changes to help inner-city families flourish, we can work together to strengthen the bond of these families and better our society as a whole.

References

Cardwell, J (2009, July 14). "Victim says prisoner will kill if released" *Akron Beacon Journal.* Retrieved September 14, 2010, from http://www.ohio.com/news/50794677.html

CBS News (2008, February 15). "Ex-cop Guilty of Murdering Pregnant Lover." Retrieved September 2, 2010, from http://www.cbsnews.com/stories/2008/02/15/national/main3836561.shtml

Cincinnati.com (2009, December 09). *The Enquirer.* "Jogger drowned, examiner rules." Retrieved August 8, 2010, from http://enquirer.com/editions/2000/12/09/loc_tristate_am_report.html

Corrigan, J. and Tinsley, J. (2008, July 13). "Twinsburg mourns officer killed in the line of duty." *Cleveland Plain Dealer.* Retrieved September 20, 2010, from http://blog.cleveland.com/metro/2008/07/twinsburg_officer_shot_killed.html

Cronin, M. and Prud, A. (1991, August 12). "Milwaukee Murders: Did They All Have to Die?" *Time.com* Retrieved October 1, 2010, from http://www.time.com/time/magazine/article/0,9171,973592,00.html

"Honoring Officers Killed in 2009." *The Officer Down Memorial Page, Inc: Remembering all of law enforcement's heroes*. Retrieved August 8, 2010, from http://www.odmp.org/year.php?year=2009&submit=go

Hoover, S. (2010). "Convicted Killer Bobby Cutts appeals to US Supreme Court." *CantonRep.com*. Retrieved September 14, 2010, from http://www.cantorep.com/news/x1664771435/Murderer-Bobby-Cutts-appeals-to-Supreme-Court

IPaer (2009, December 5). MS-13. Gang Altered Dimensions. net. Retrieved October 2, 2010 from http://www.altereddimensions.net/crime/ms13gang.aspx

Juror Thirteen (2010). The Bobby Cutts Murder Case. Retrieved July 21, 2010, from http://www.jurorthirteen.com/TheBobbyCuttsCase/tabid/69/default.aspx

Kropko, M. (2005, December 3). "Gehring children's bodies identified" *Concord Monitor.* Retrieved September 4,

2010, from www.concordmonitor.com/article/gehring-childrens-bodies-identified

Leniham, E. (2009, February 19). "Muslim community knew of Hassan's abuse." *WIVB-TV.* Retrieved September 26, 2010, from http://www.wivb.com/dpp/news/Muslim_community_knew_of_Hassans_abuse_20090219

Mansfield, E. (Host, 2010) "Doug Parade failed polygraph test after murder." *WKYC-TV.* Retrieved September 8, 2010, from http://www.wkyc.com/print.aspx?storyid=78409

Meyer, E. (2010, May 5). "High court sends Prade case back to Summit County." *Akron Beacon Journal.* Retrieved July 12, 2010 from http://allbusiness.com/crime-law-enforcement-corrections/law-forensics-Forensic/14393416-1.html

Miller, D. (1998, September 24). "Prade Convicted in Slaying of Ex-wife." *Cleveland Plain Dealer.* Retrieved August 4, 2010, from http://blog.cleveland.com/pdextra/2009/06/prade_convicted_in_slaying_of.html

Murungi, M. (Host, 2010). "Compton United Field of Dreams or Lack Thereof." *Nutmeg Radio.* Retrieved September 17, 2010, from http://www.nutmegradio.com/compton-uniteds-field-of-dreams-or-lack-thereof/

Nethers, D. (2010, May 25). "Officer Murder Trial, Day 2: Officers Recall Shooting Night." *Fox 8 News*. Retrieved September 21, 2010, from http://www.fox8.com/news/wjw-news-officer-Miktarian-murder-trial-day-two,0,2916280. story

Palmer, P. (Host-2006, August 01). *KABC-TV.* Los Angeles, CA [Television News Episode]. "Gang Member Gets 82 Years to Life." [Transcript] Retrieved June 21, 2010, from http://abclocal.go.com/kabc/story?section=news/local&id=4421309

Police Officer Divorce Data (2010). *HeavyBadge.com* Retrieved September 3, 2010, from http://www.heavybadge. com/efstress.html

Ravitz, J. (2009, April 8). "Out-of-wedlock births hit record high." *CNN Living*. Retrieved September 2, 2010, from http://articles.cnn.com/2009-0408/living/out.of.wedlock. births_1_out-of-wedlock-unwed-mothers-wedding-dress/2?_s=PM:LIVING

Sabol, W. (2008, June). Bureau of Justice Statistics, Prison Inmates at Midyear 2007. *Washington, DC: US Department of Justice,* June 2008. Retrieved September 1, 2010, from http://www.drugwarfacts.org/cms/node/64

Snyder, H. (2001, December). "Law Enforcement and Juvenile Crime Juvenile Offenders and Victims." *National Report Series, pp. 10-14.* Retrieved June 14, 2010, from http://ncjrs.gov/pdffiles1/ojjdp/191031.pdf

Sperling's Best Places. (2010, Statistics). *Akron, Ohio Race and Ethnicity [Pie Chart].* Retrieved August 5, 2010, from http://bestplaces.net/city/Akron-Ohio.aspx#

Stockinger, J. (2010, September 8). "Priest gets 4 years for molesting St. Charles boy." *Daily Herald.* Retrieved September 10, 2010, from http://www.dailyherald.com/story/?id406562

Terry, D. (1994, November 29). "Jeffrey Dahmer, Multiple Killer, Is Bludgeoned to Death in Prison." The New York Times. Retrieved October 1, 2010, from http://www.nytimes.com/1994/11/29/us/jeffrey-dahmer-multiple-killer-is-bludgeoned-to-death-in-prison.html?pagewanted=all

Thompson, C. (2009, February 17). "Accused of Beheading Wife in NY May Have Committed 'Honor Killing'." The Huffington Post. Retrieved September 27, 2010, from http://www.huffingtonpost.com/2009/02/17/muzzammil-hassan-muslim-t_n_167772.html

Toppo, G. (2009, April 14). "10 years later, the real story behind Columbine." *USA Today.* Retrieved June 23, 2010, from http://www.usatoday.com/news/nation/2009-04-13-columbine-myths_N.html

Tacking Officers' PTSD (2010). *The Badge of Life.* "Psychological Survival for Police Police Officers." Retrieved September 28, 2010, from http://badgeoflife.com/currentmyths.php

Tracking Police Suicides (2008, 2009). *The Badge of Life: Psychological Survival for Police Officers.* Retrieved September 1, 2010 from http://badgeoflife.com/suicides.php

Violanti, J. (1999). "Alcohol Abuse in Policing: Prevention Strategies." *The FBI Law Enforcement Bulletin.* Retrieved July 9, 2010, from http://findarticles.com/p/articles/mi_m2194/is_68/ai_54036506/

Index

Edwards Brothers,Inc!
Thorofare, NJ 08086
22 March, 2011
BA2011081